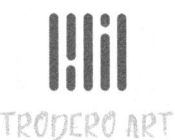

TRODERO ART

Copyright © 2020 By H. Elmir

All rights reserved. This book or parts thereof may not be reproduced in any form, stored in any retrieval system, or transmitted in any form by any means electronic, mechanical, photocopy, recording, or otherwise without prior written permission of the publisher, except as provided by United States of America copyright law.

ISBN: 9798578527968

Printed by AMAZON KDP.

First printing edition 2021.

www.amazon.com

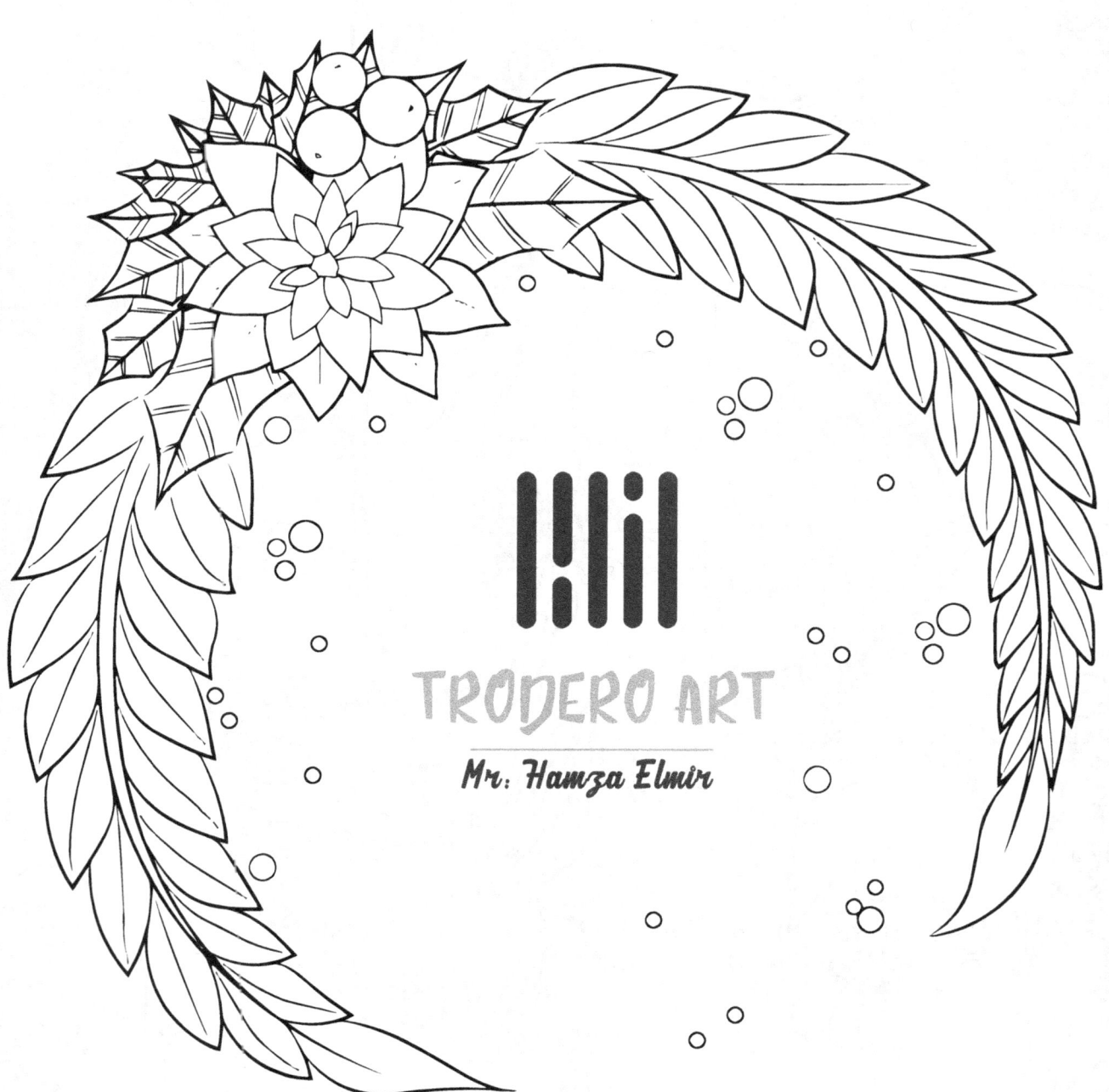

This Book Belongs To

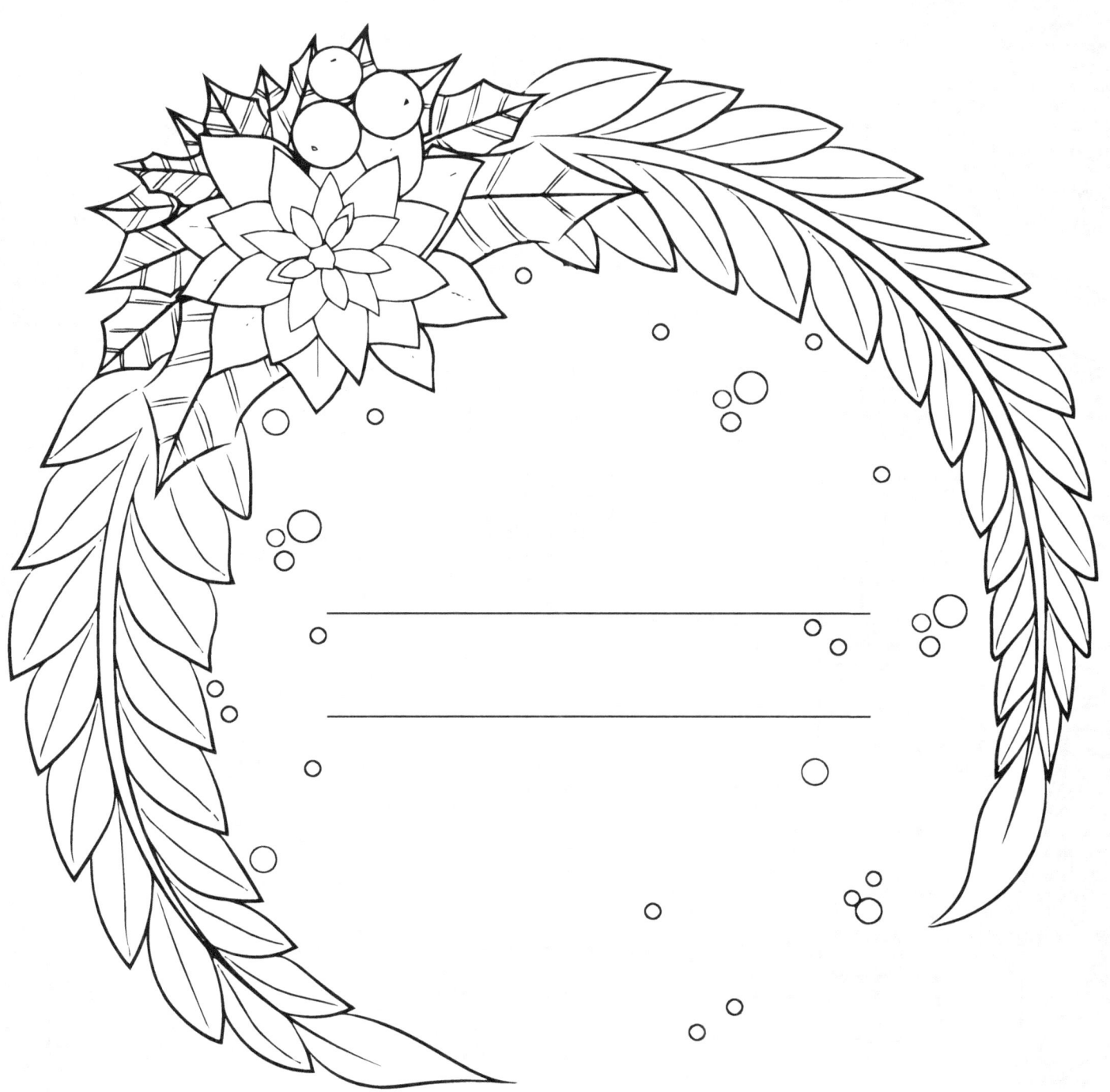

Step To a Relaxing Coloring

1. Find a quiet space. it's easier to focus on what you are doing when there are no distraction.

2. Organize your materials. Lay out your coloring book and crayons or pens.

3. Set the mood. Turn on some tranquil music, diffuse lavender or another.

4. Select your picture. Wich image speacks to you today, that's the one you should color.

5. Choose your palette. Select the colors you will be using for your image.

6. Begin coloring. This is the fun part. Don't worry about getting everything perfect, just start.

How is coloring relaxing?

Coloring has the ability to relax the fear center of your brain, the amygdala. It induces the same state as meditating by reducing the thoughts of a restless mind. This generates mindfulness and quietness, which allows your mind to get some rest after a long day at work.

Color Test Page

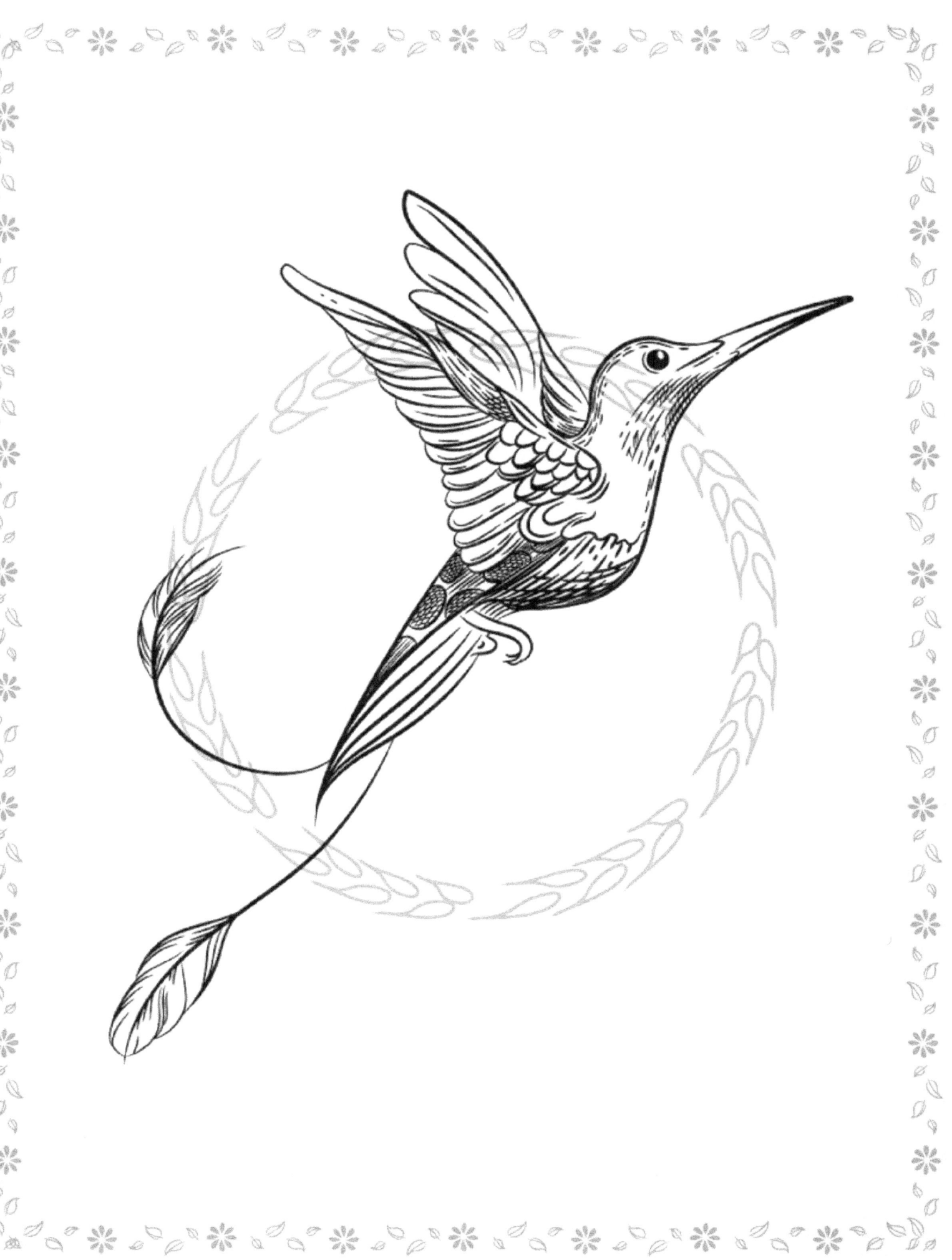

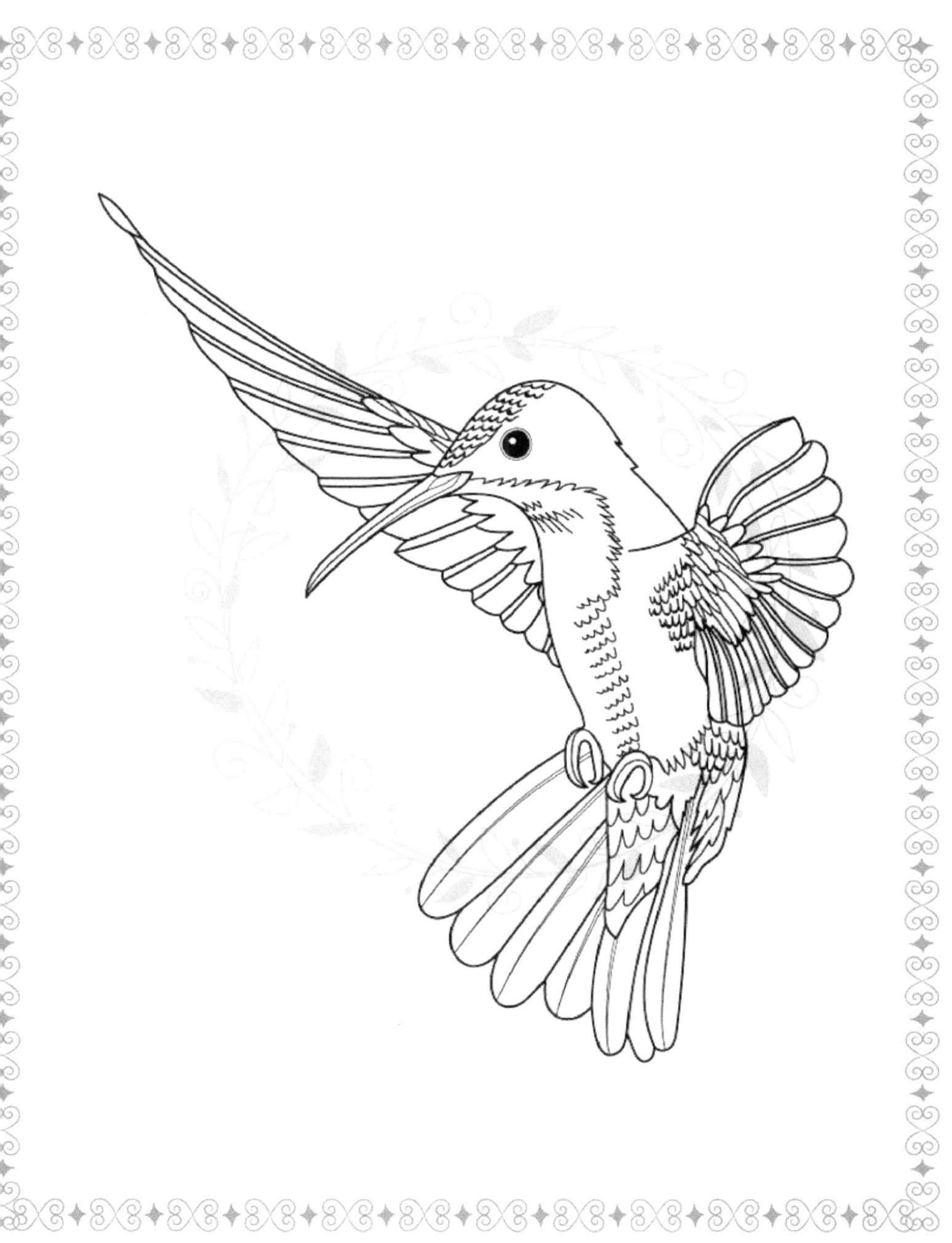

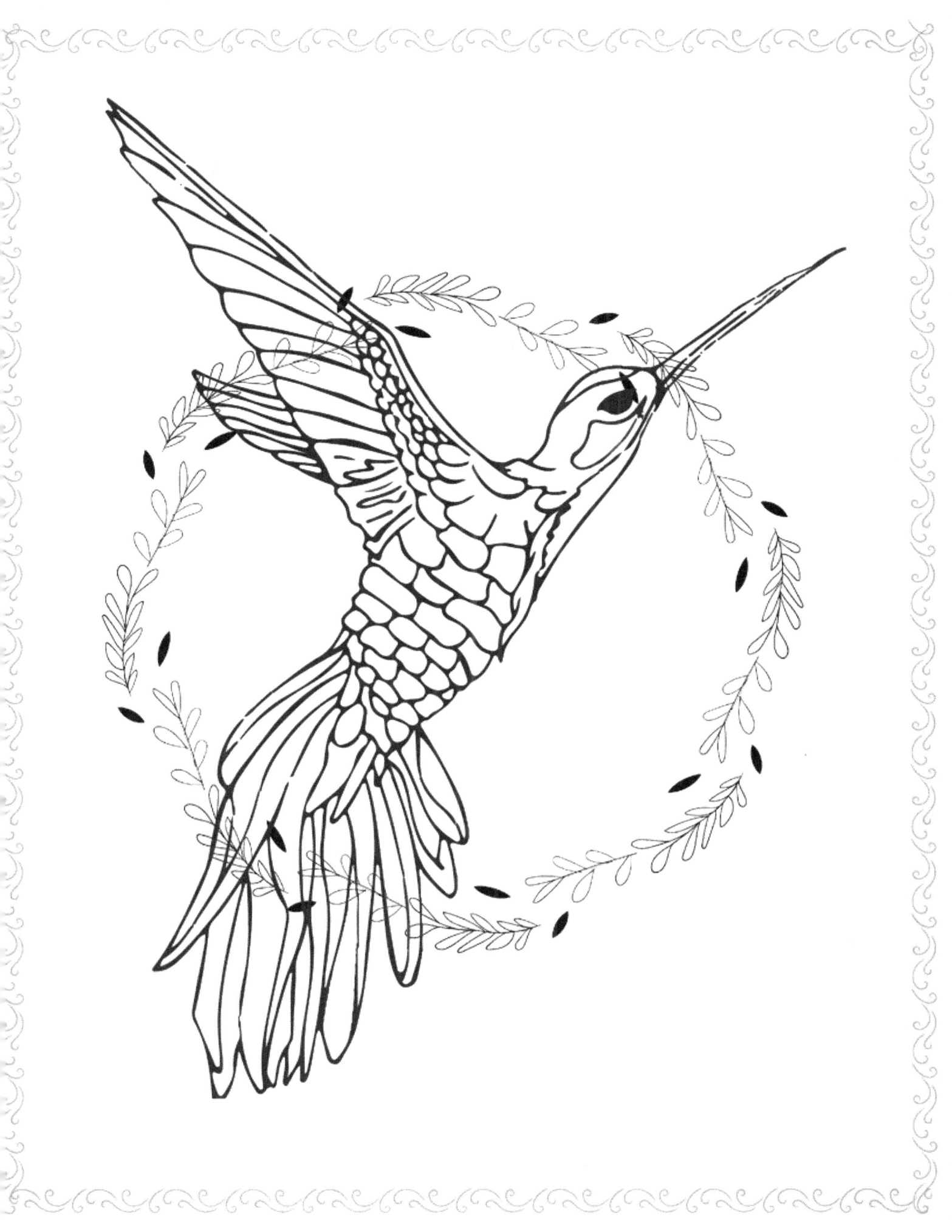

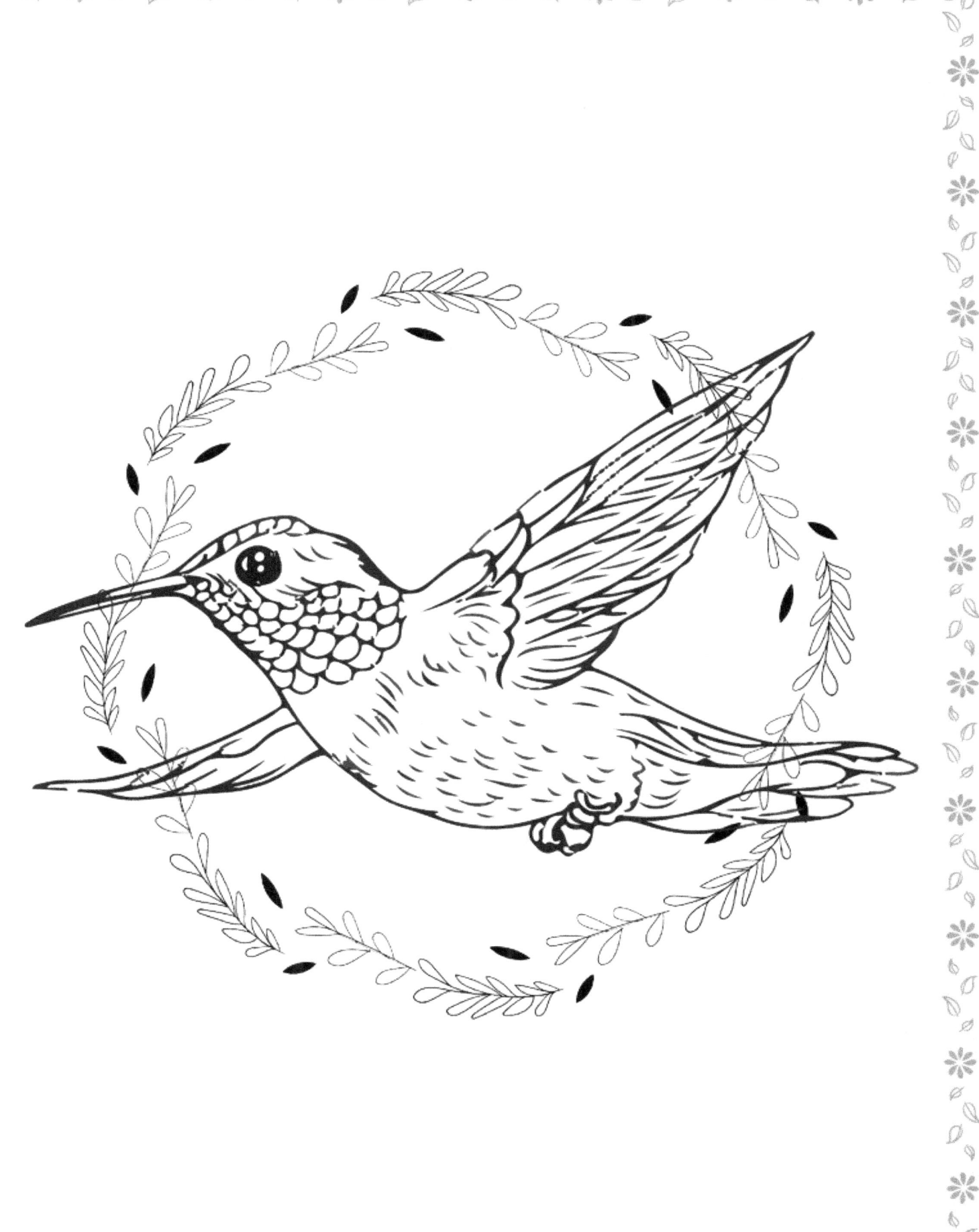

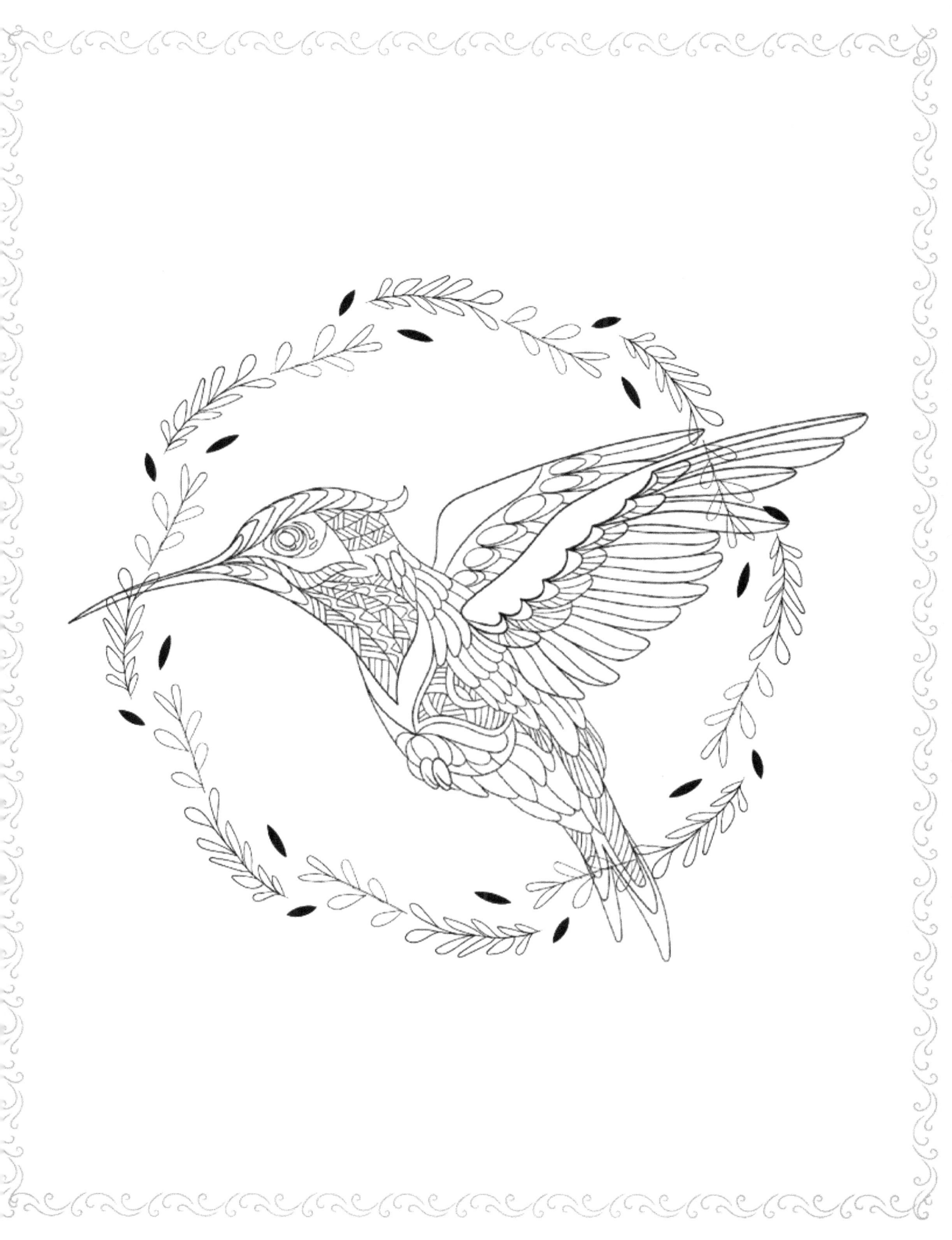

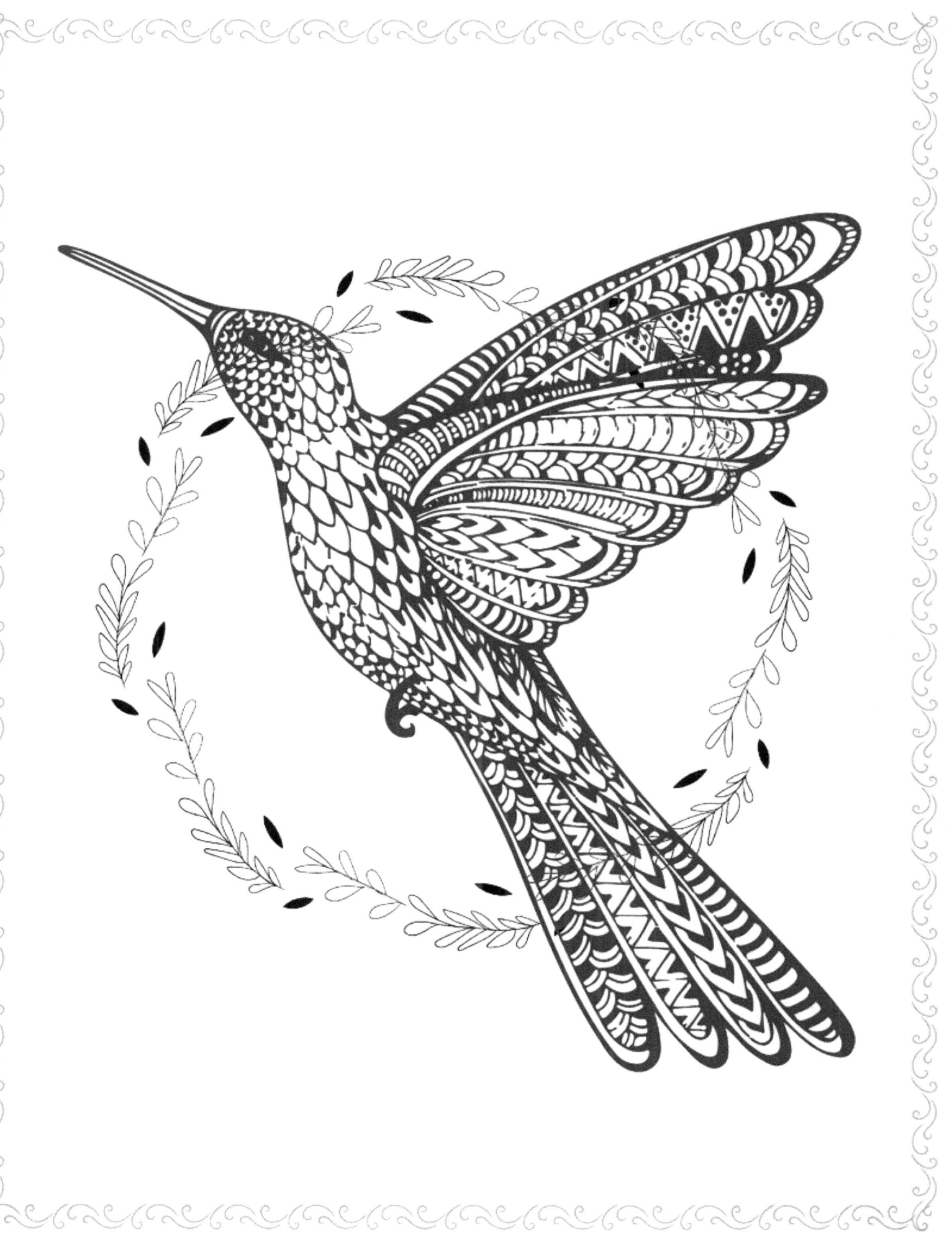

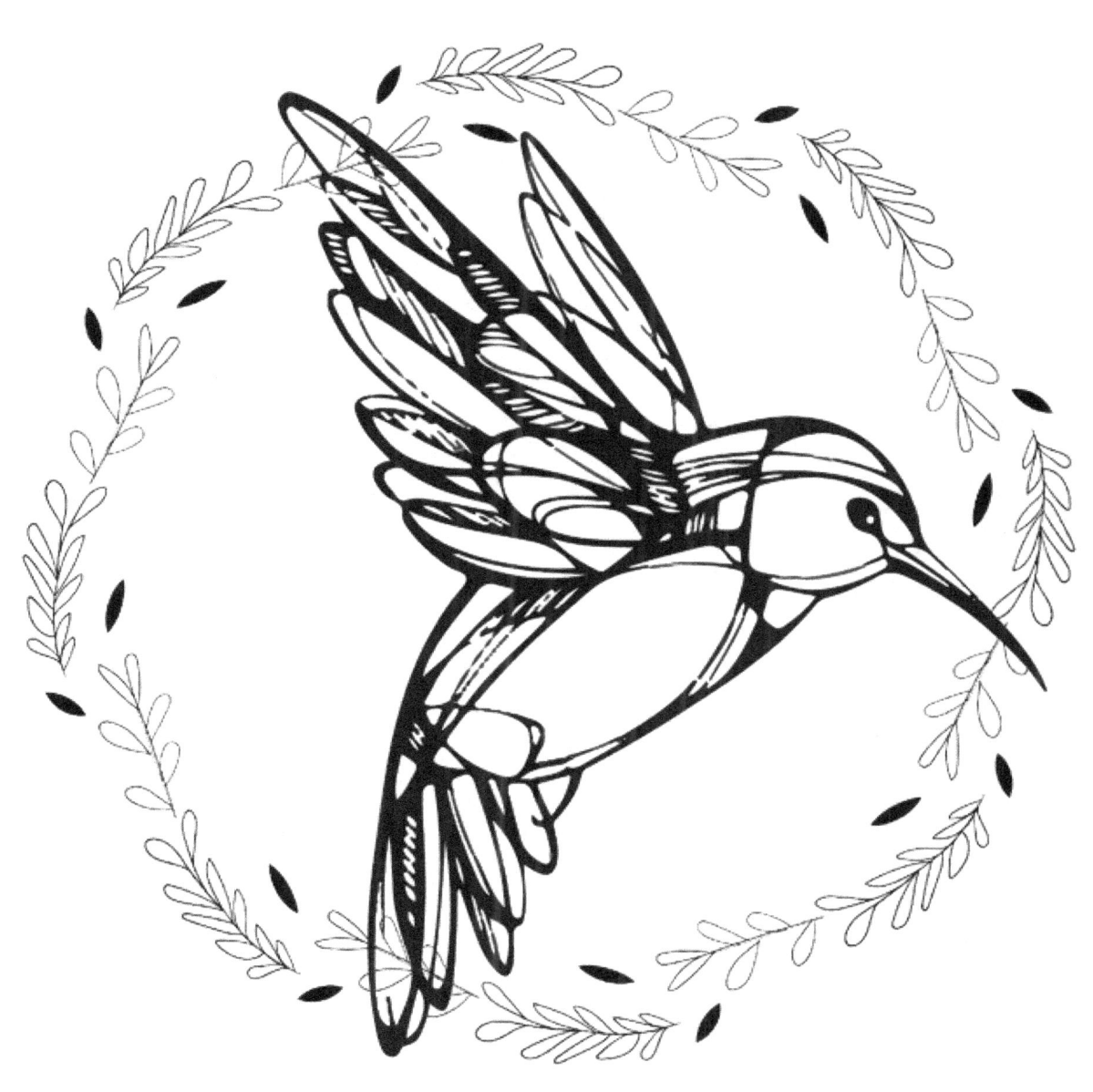

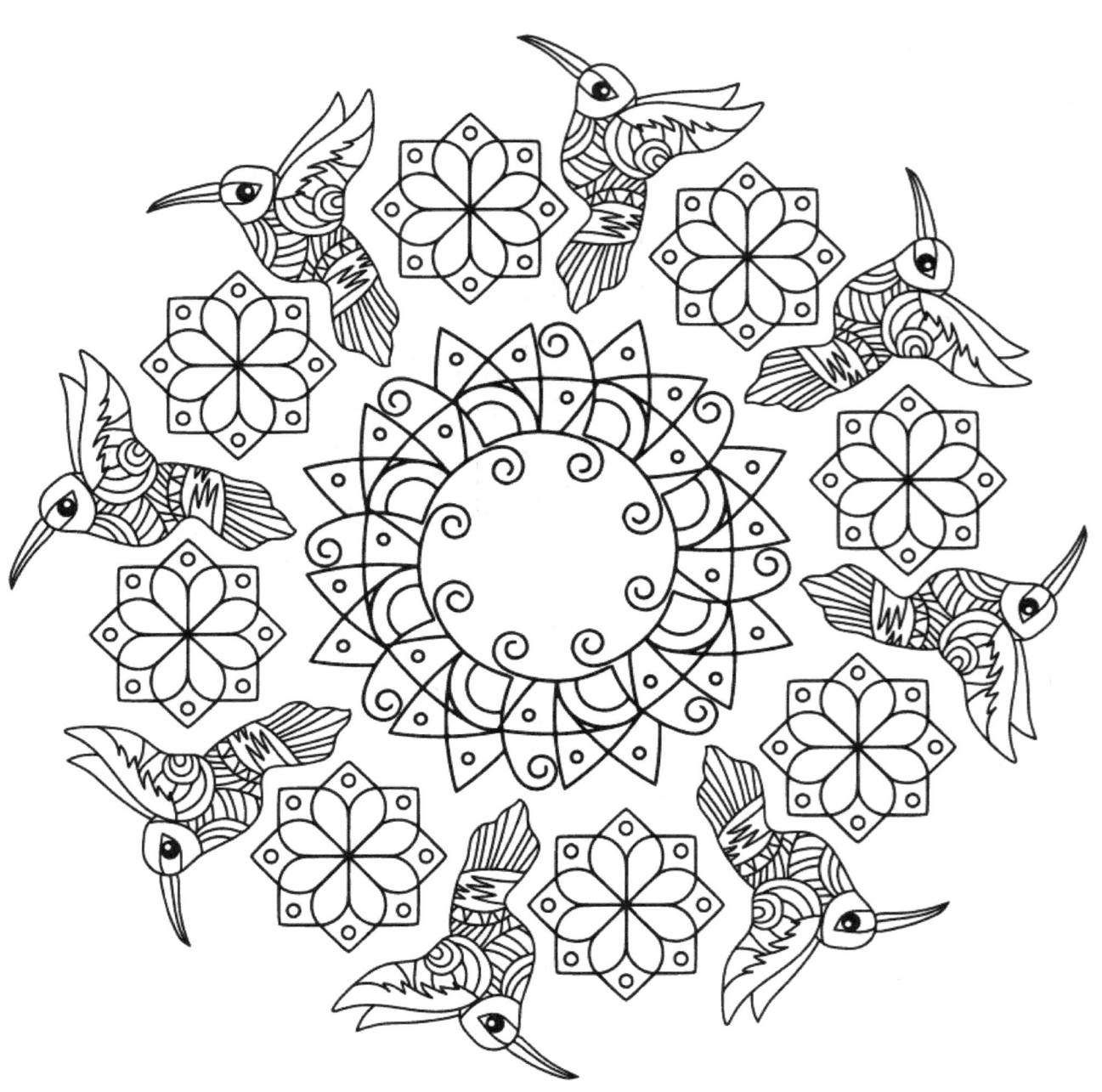

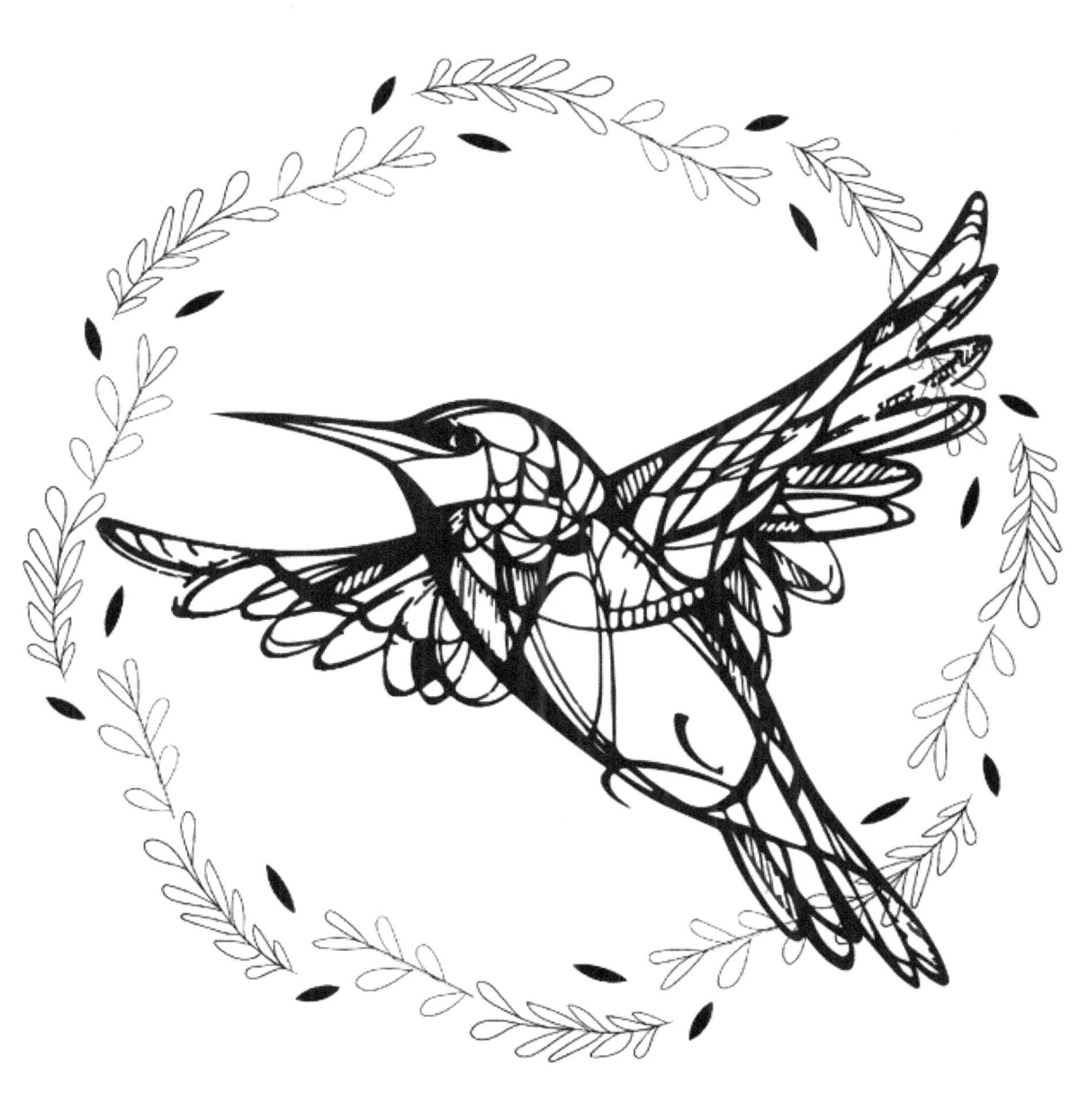

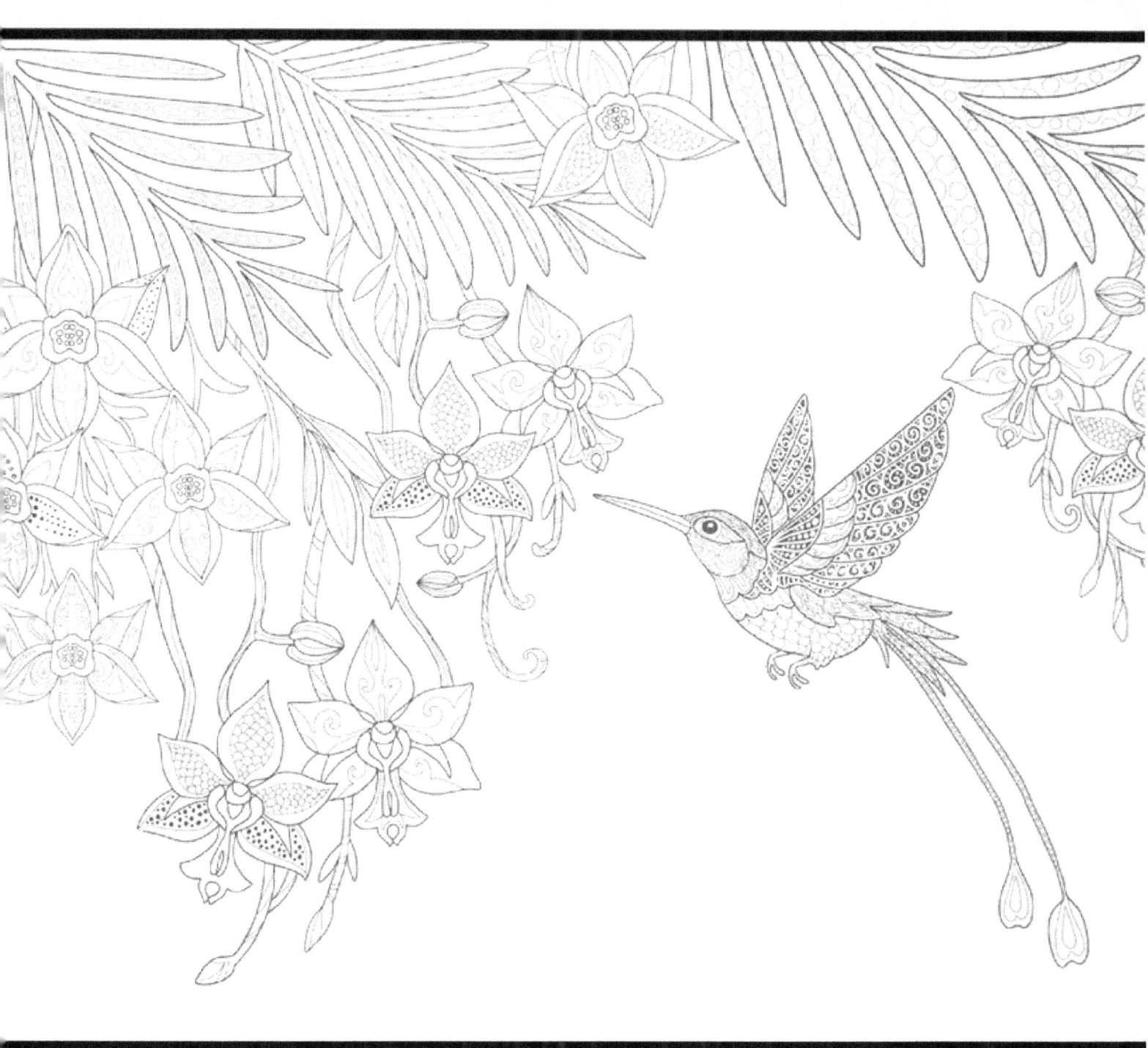

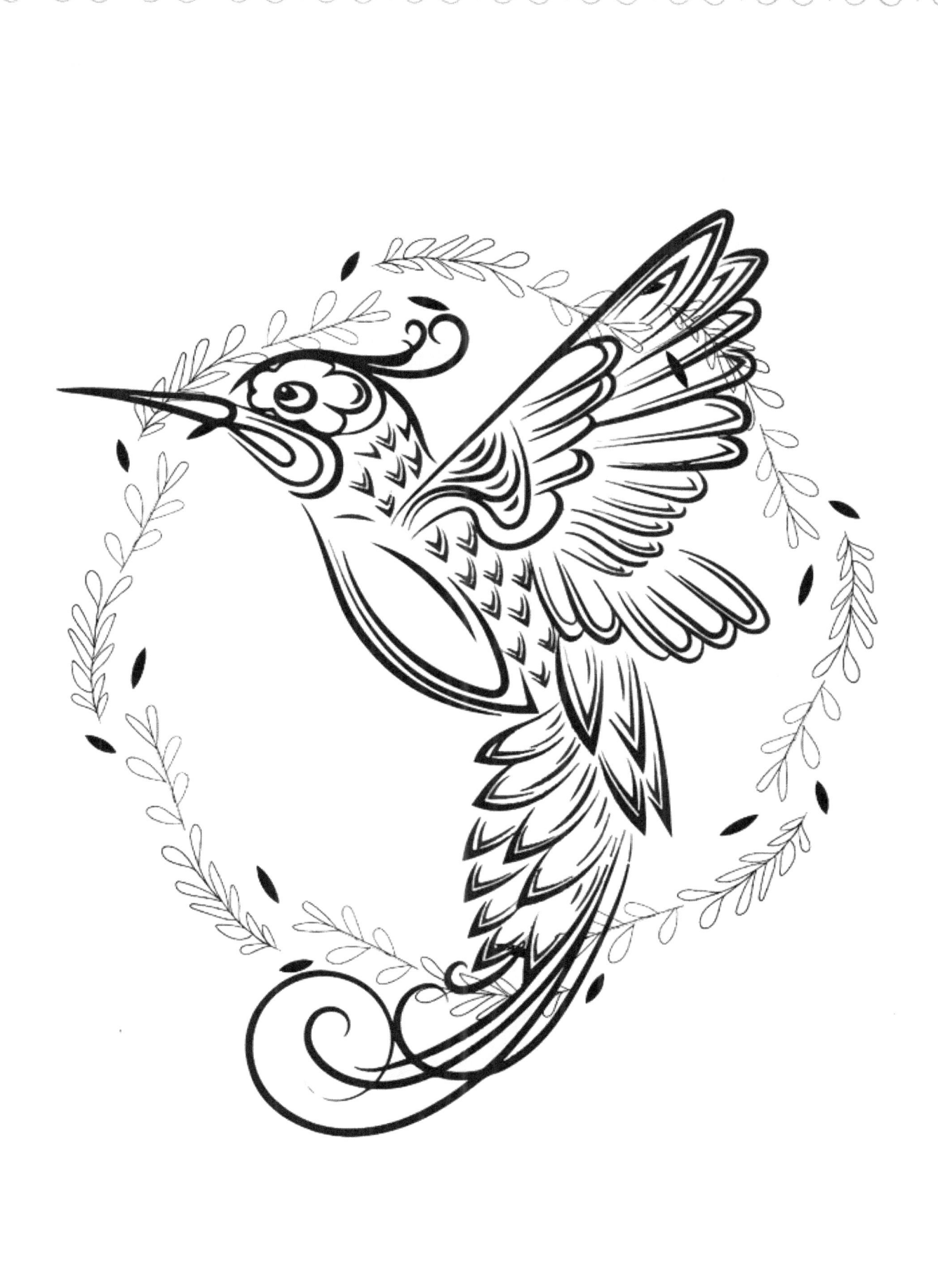

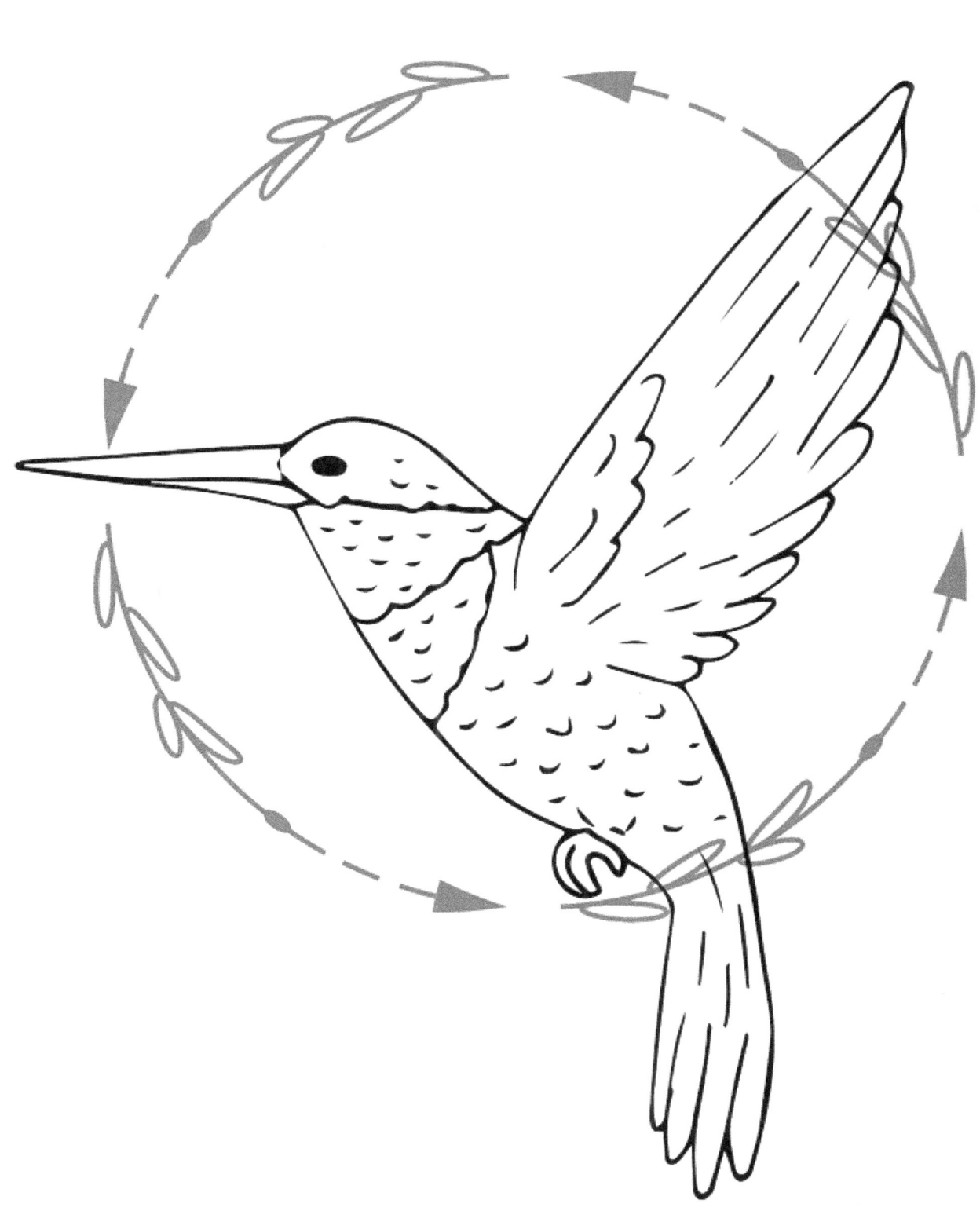

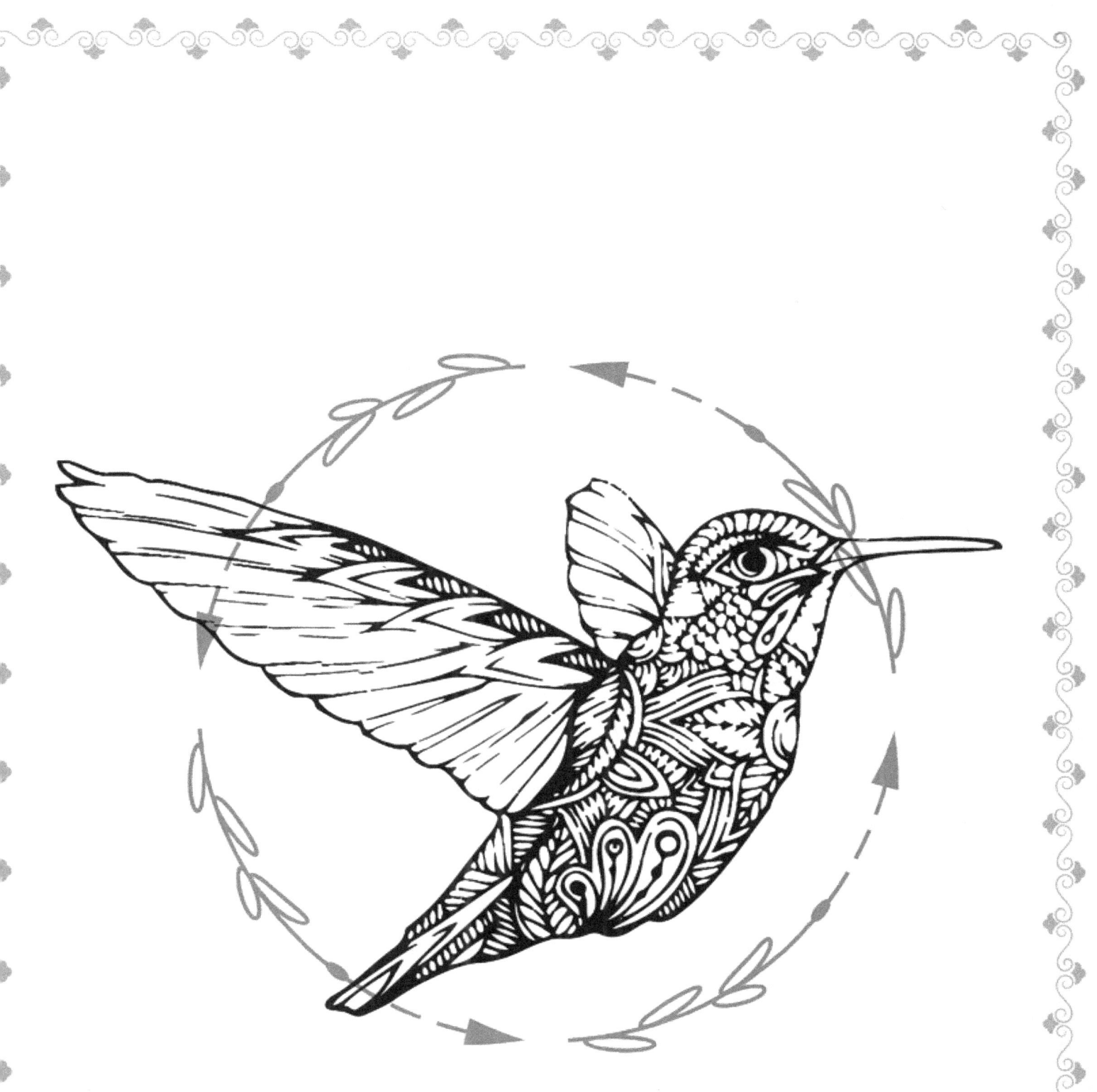

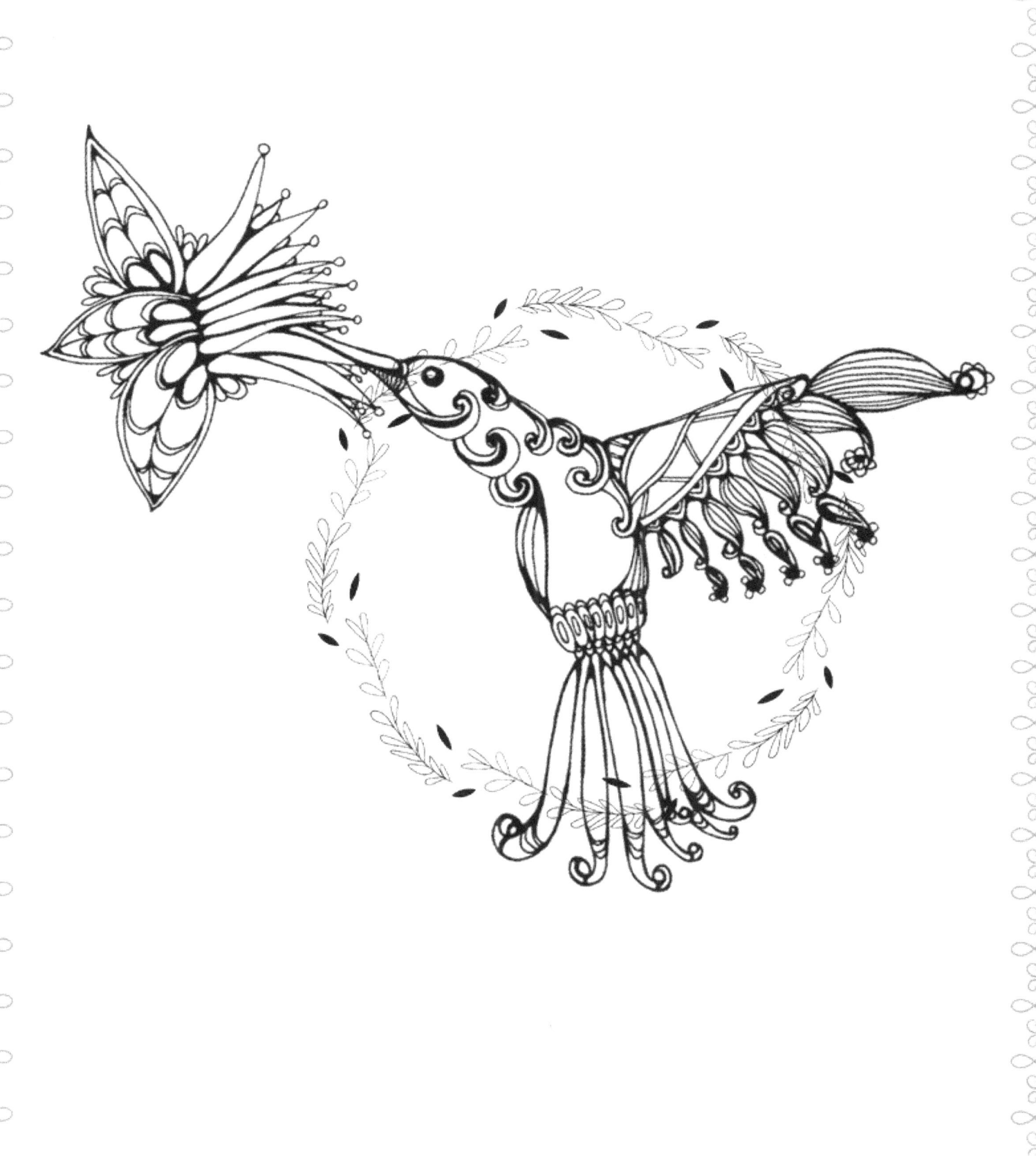

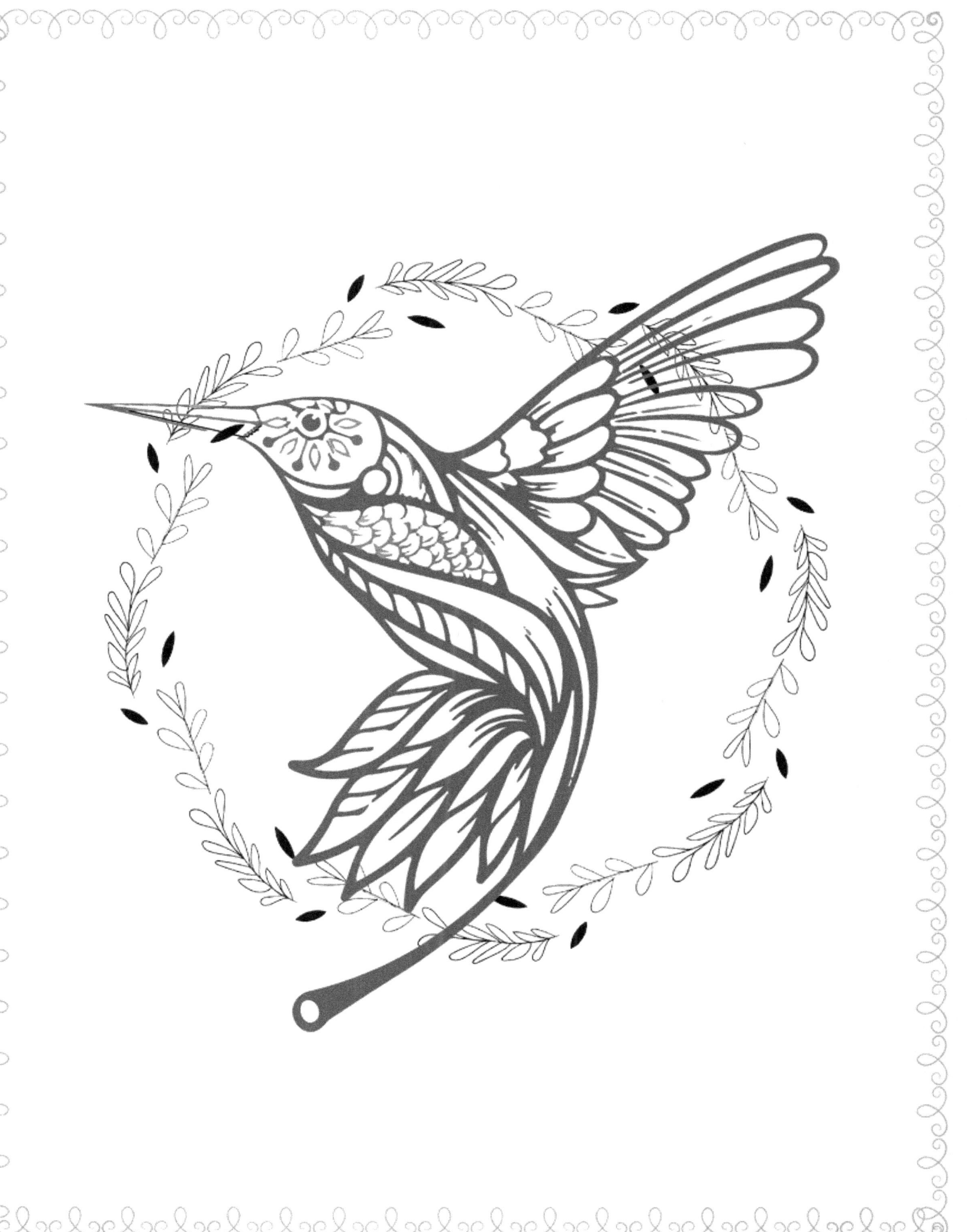

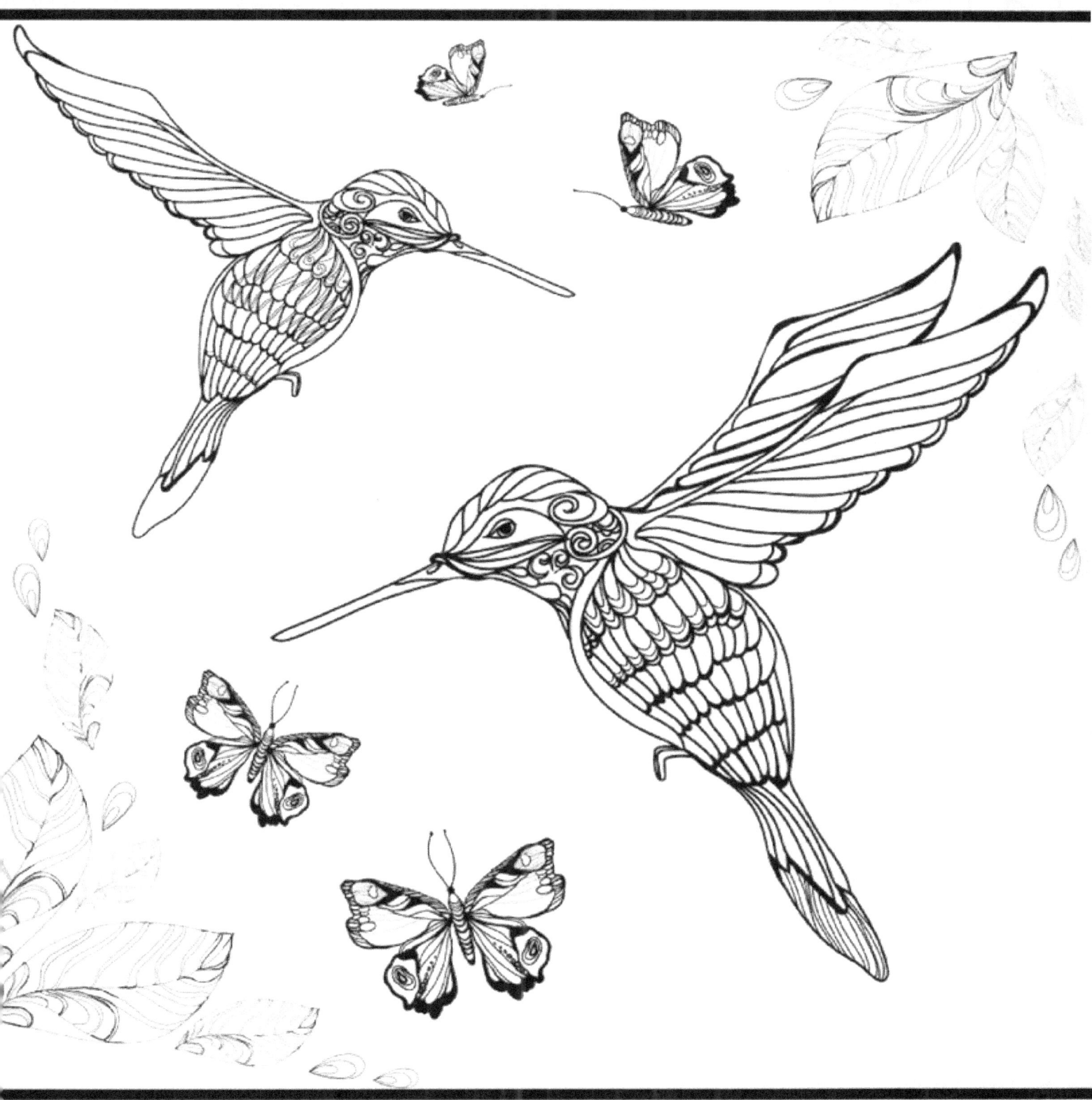

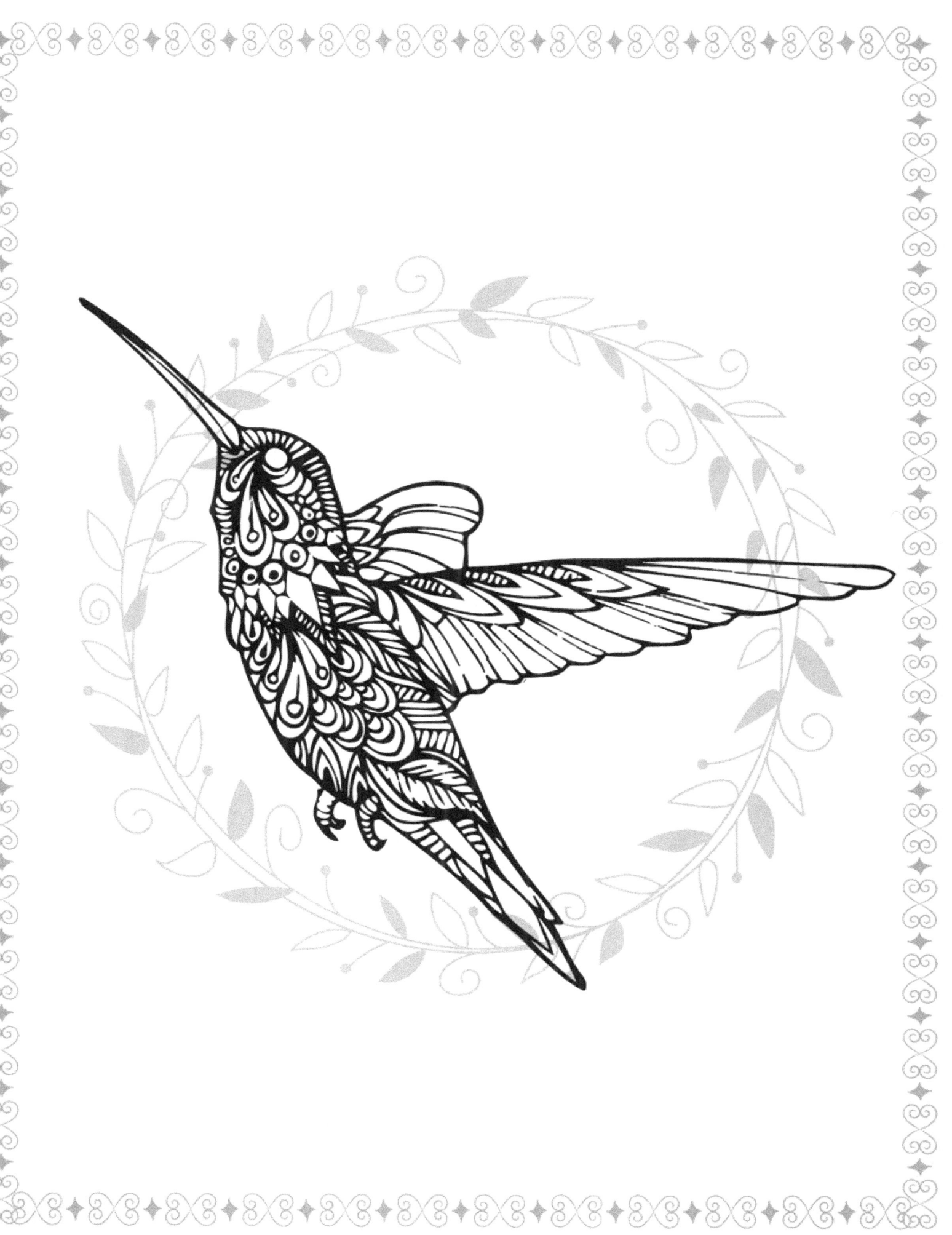

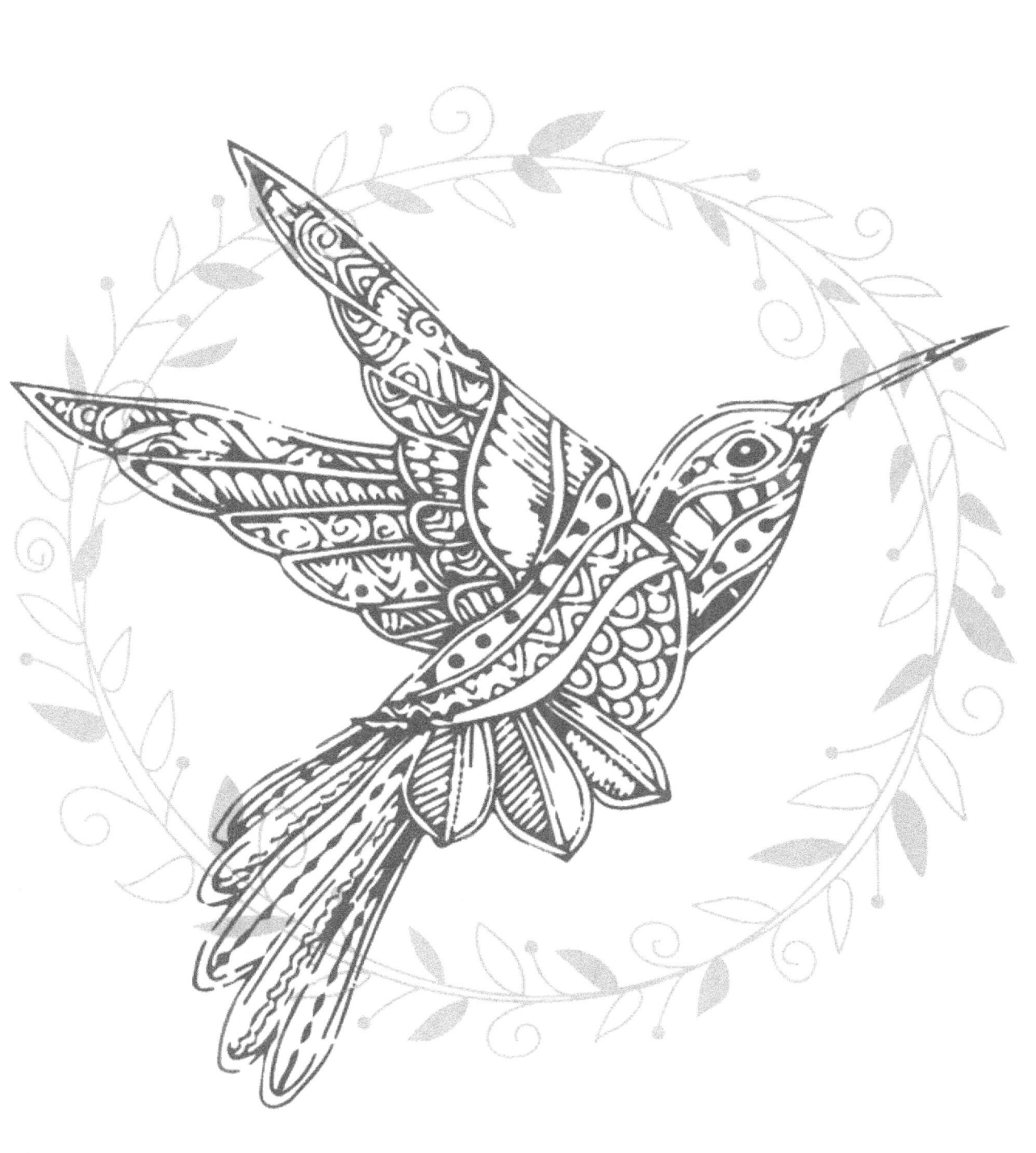

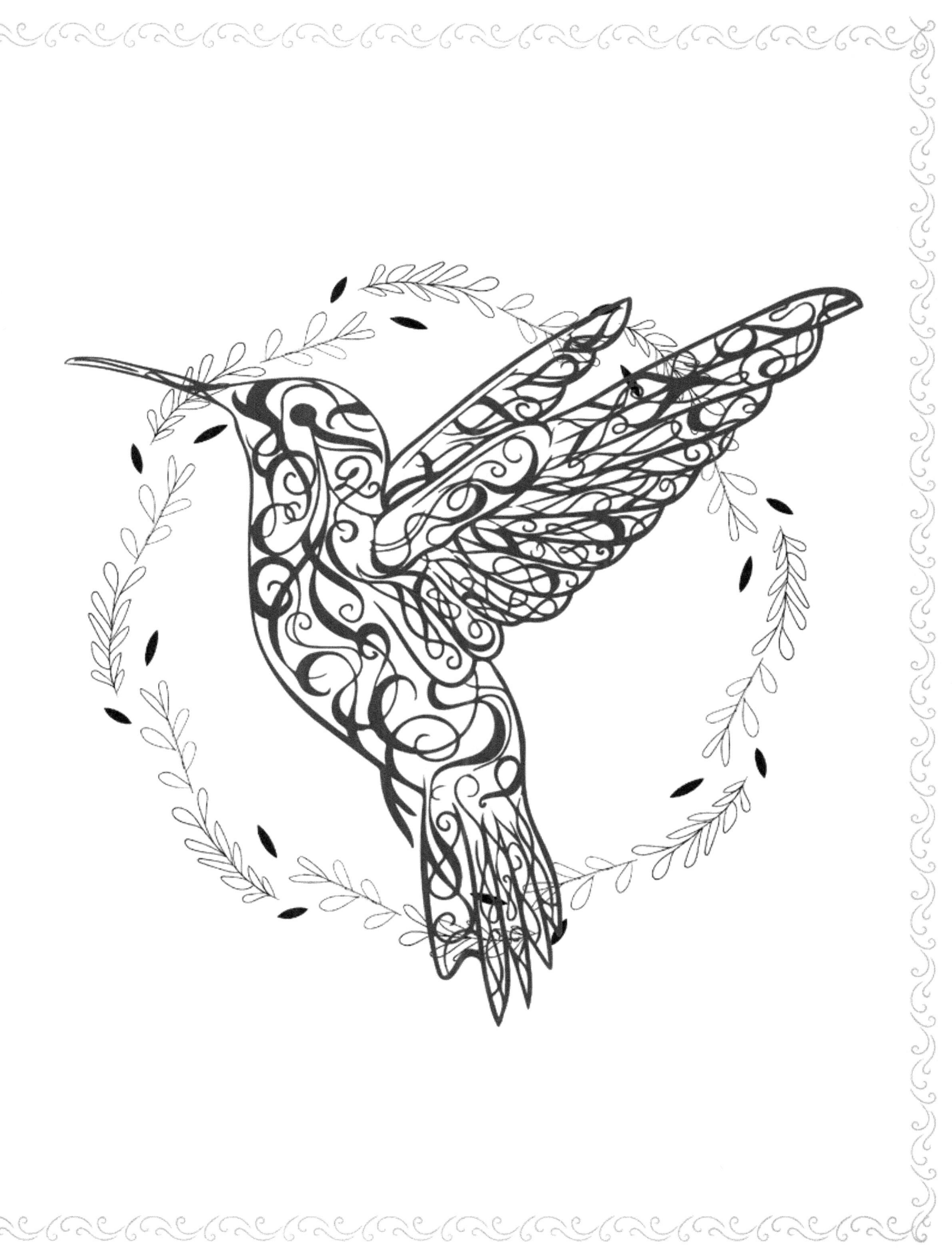

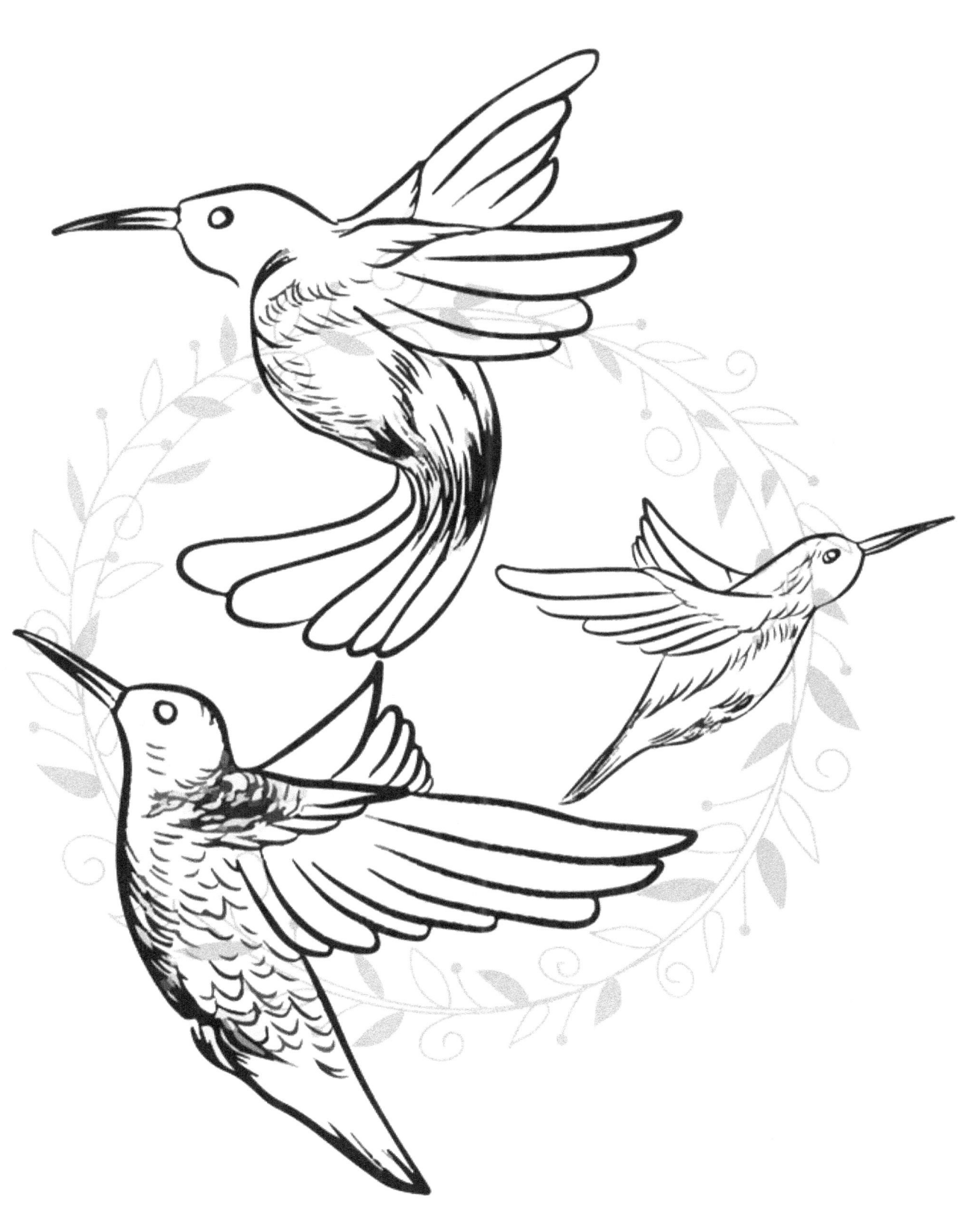

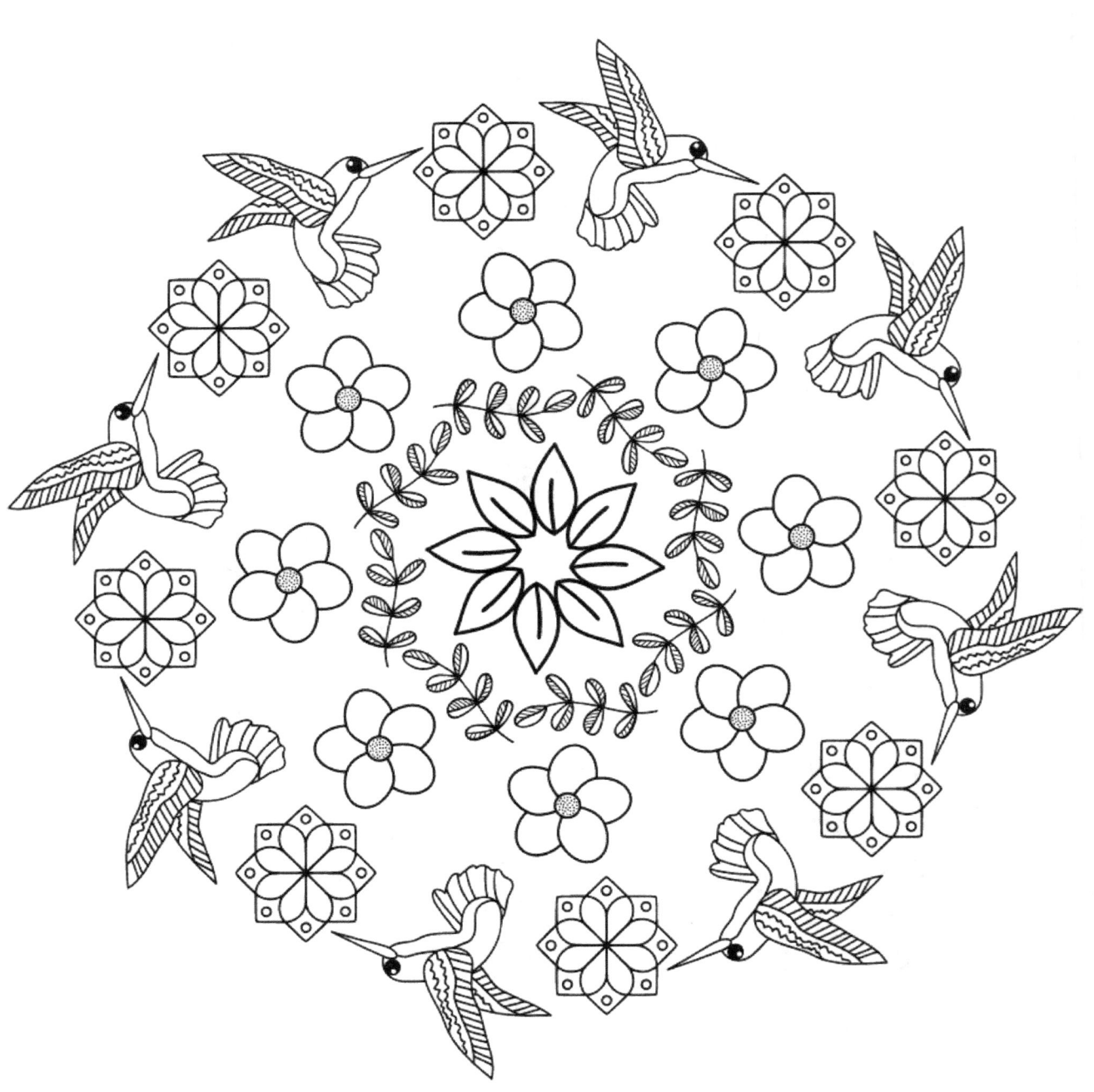

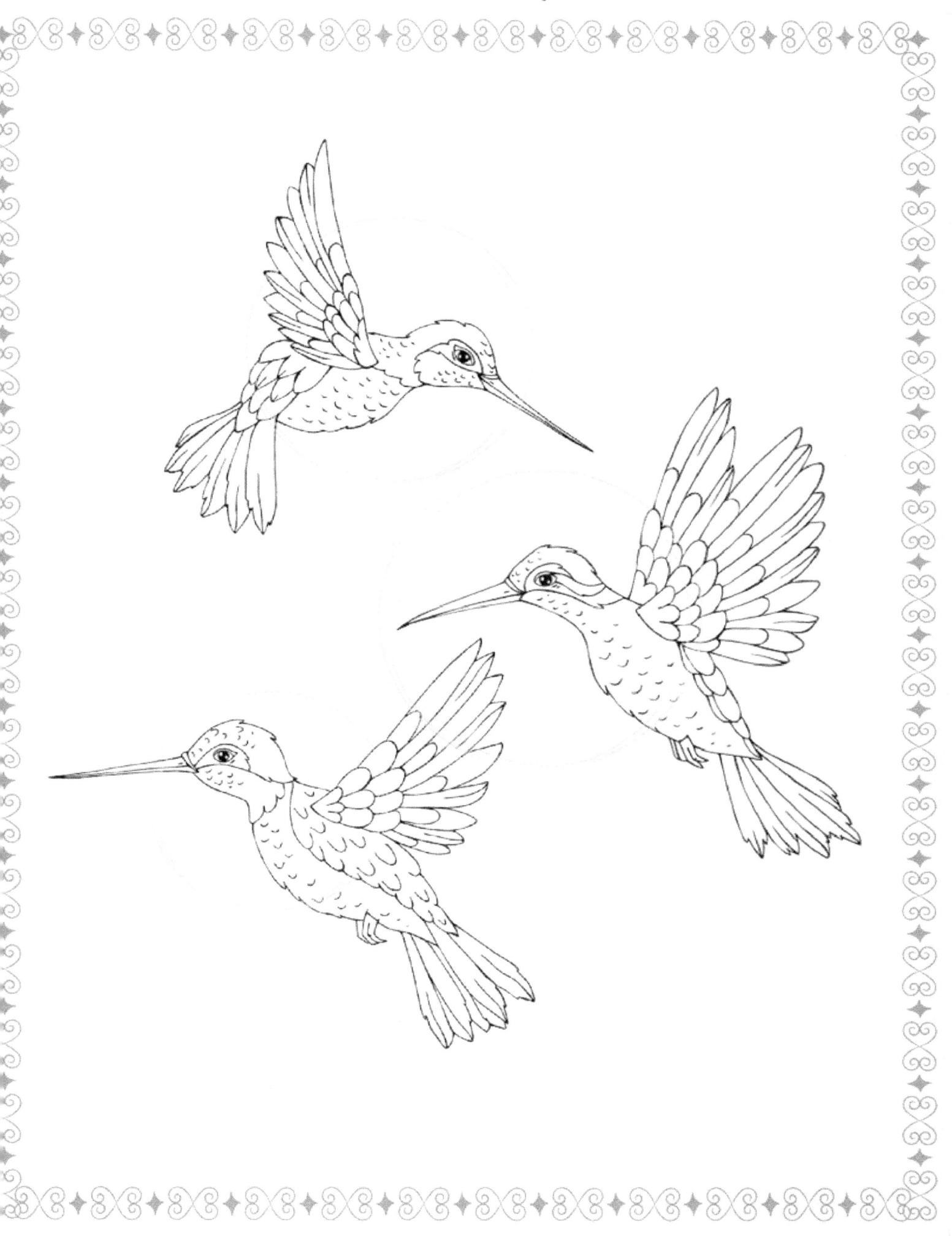

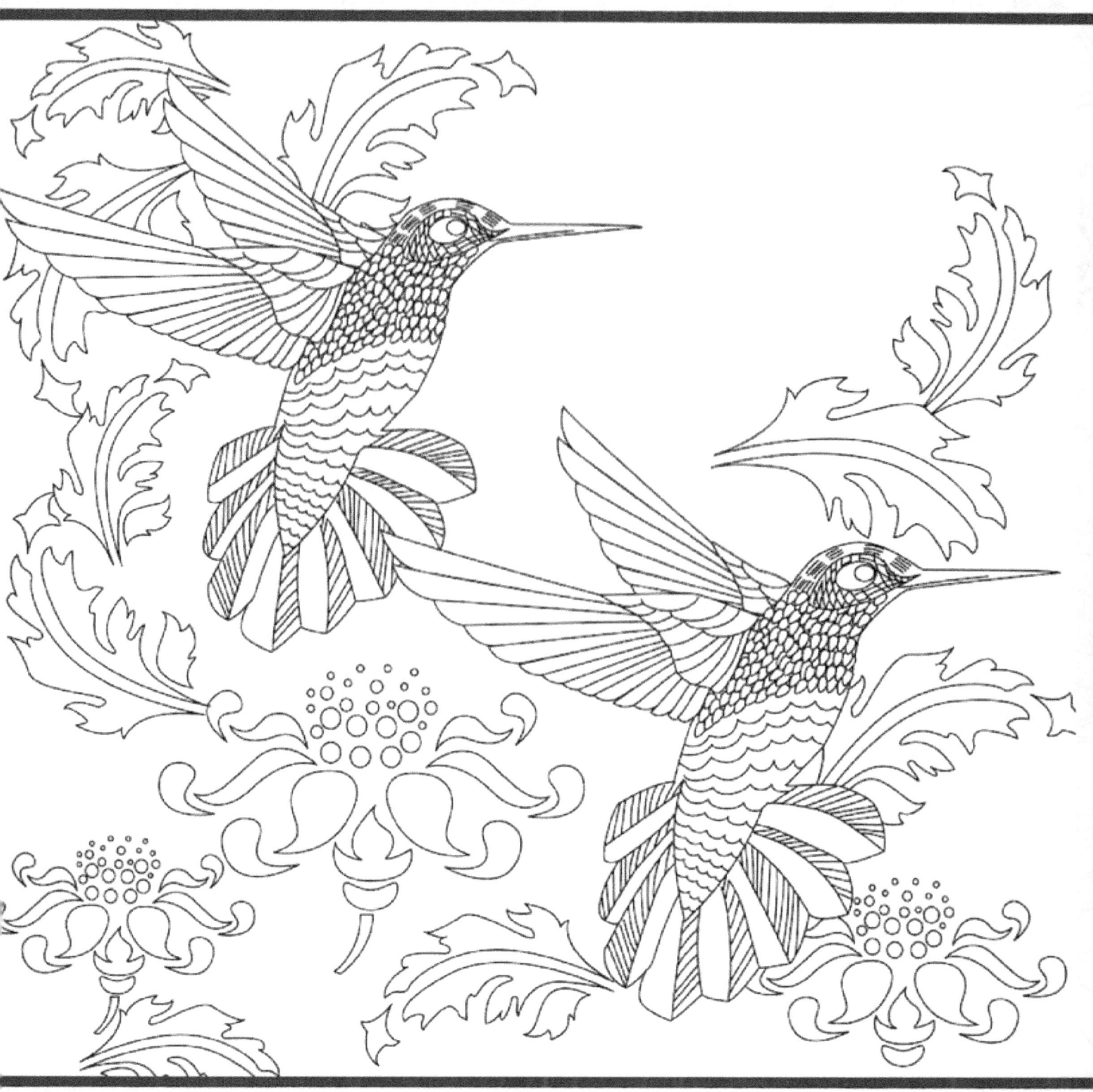

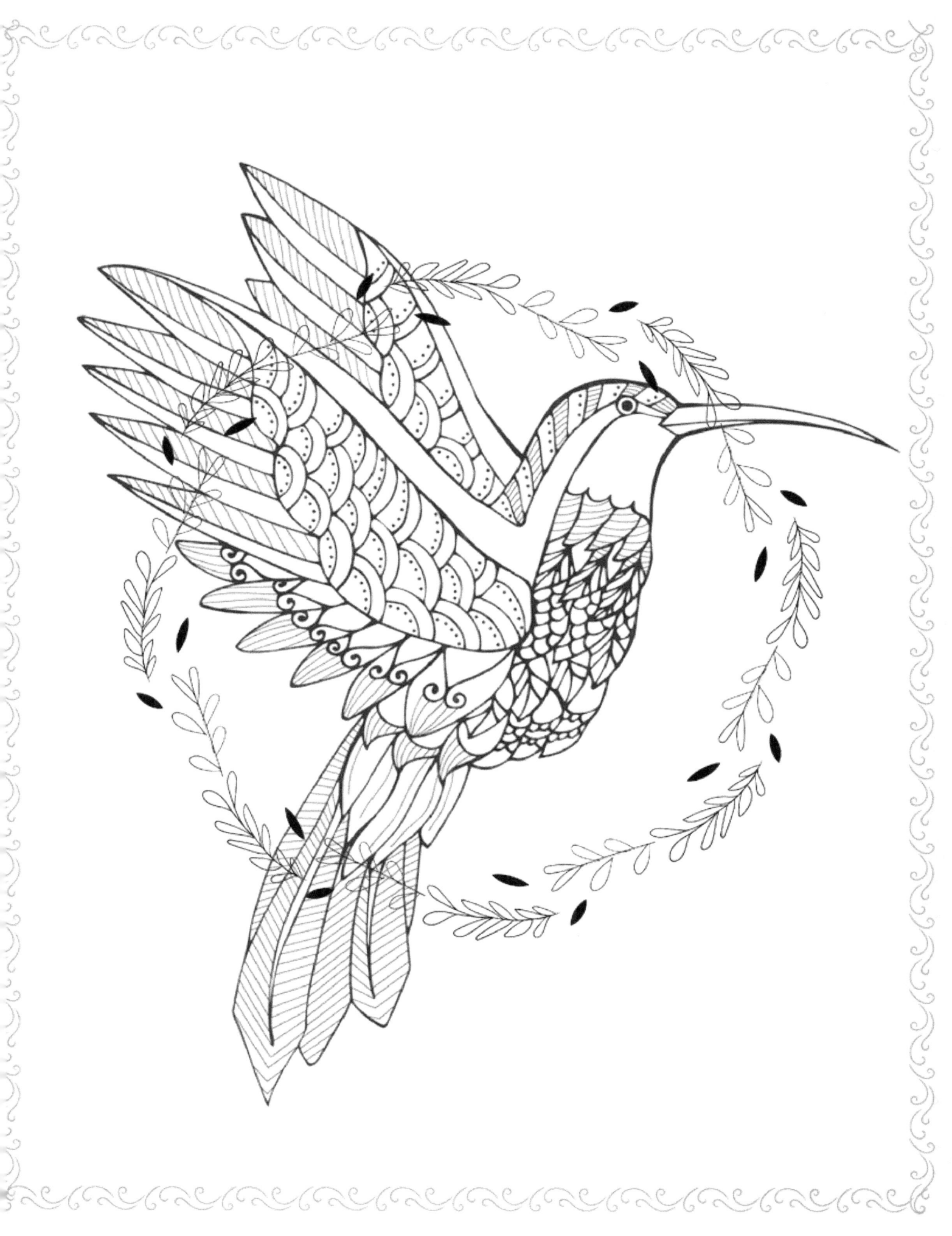

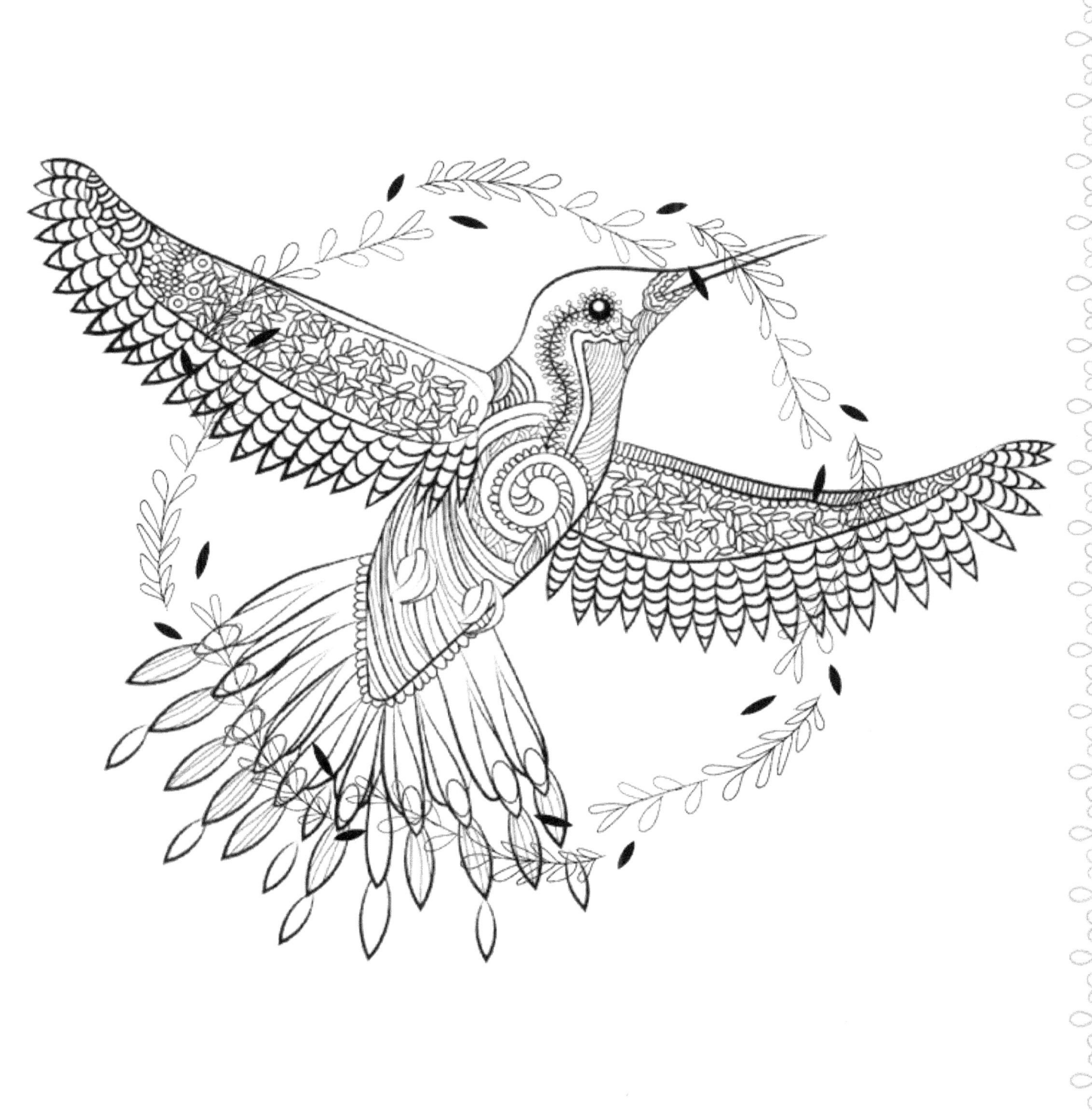

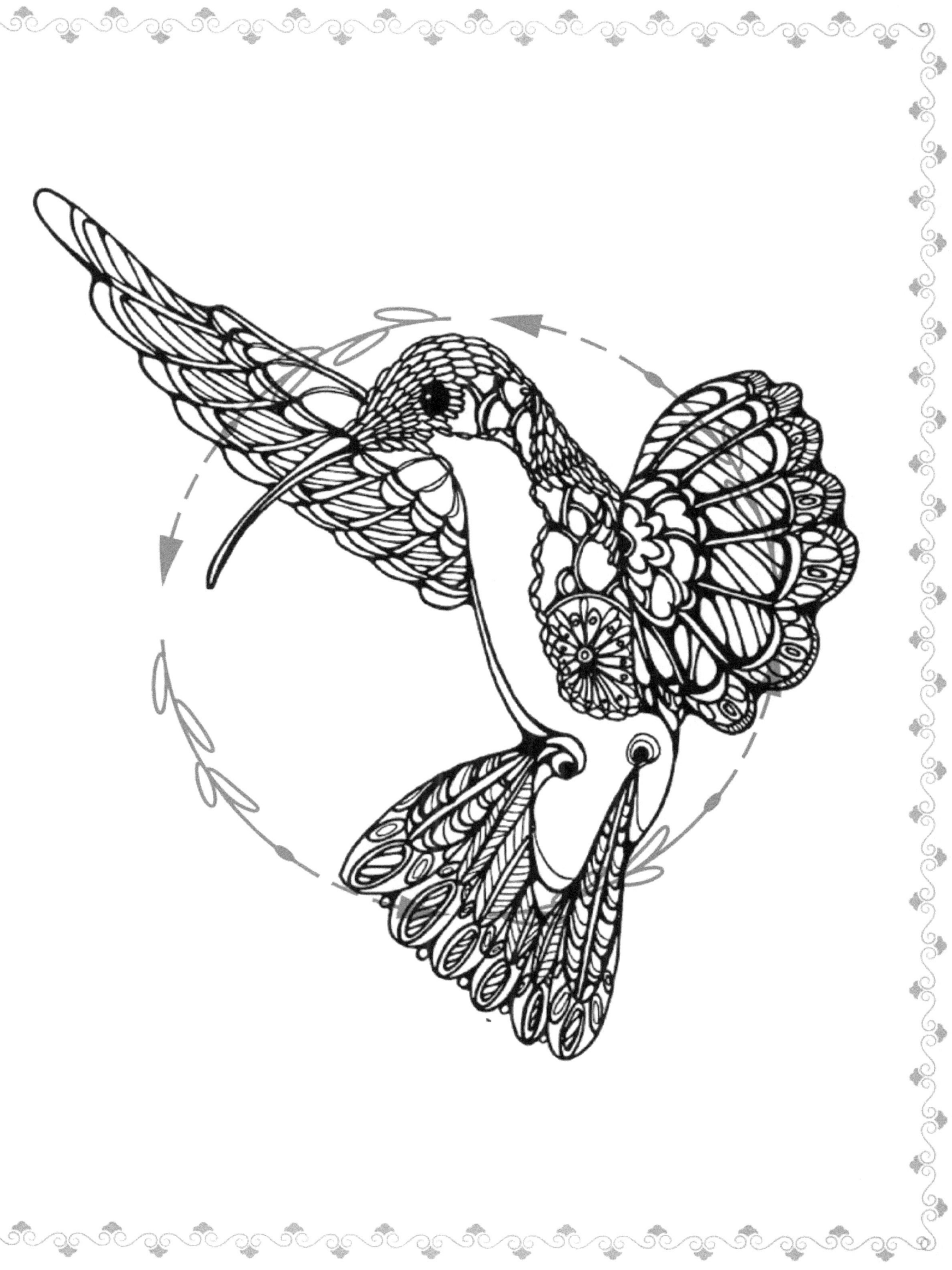

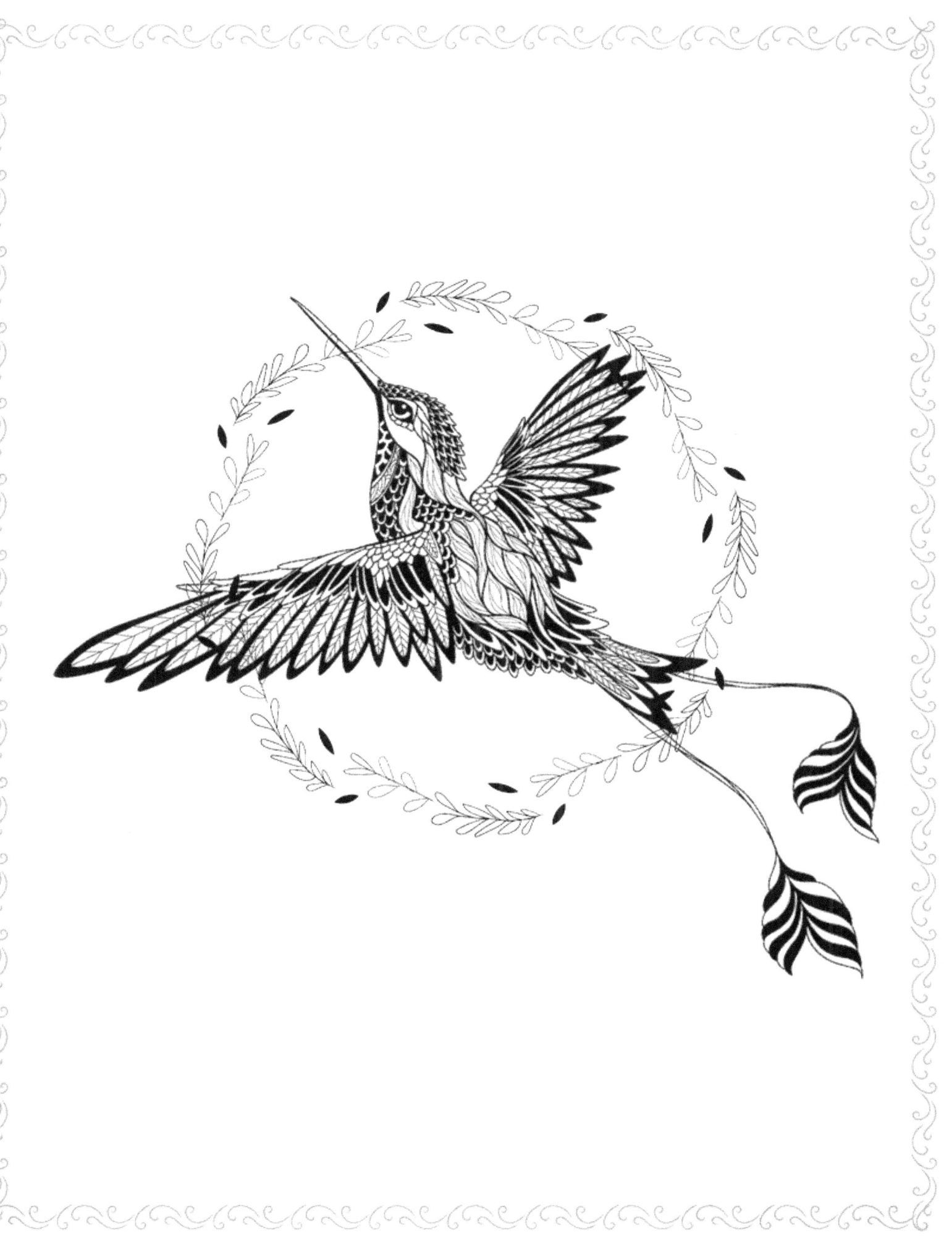

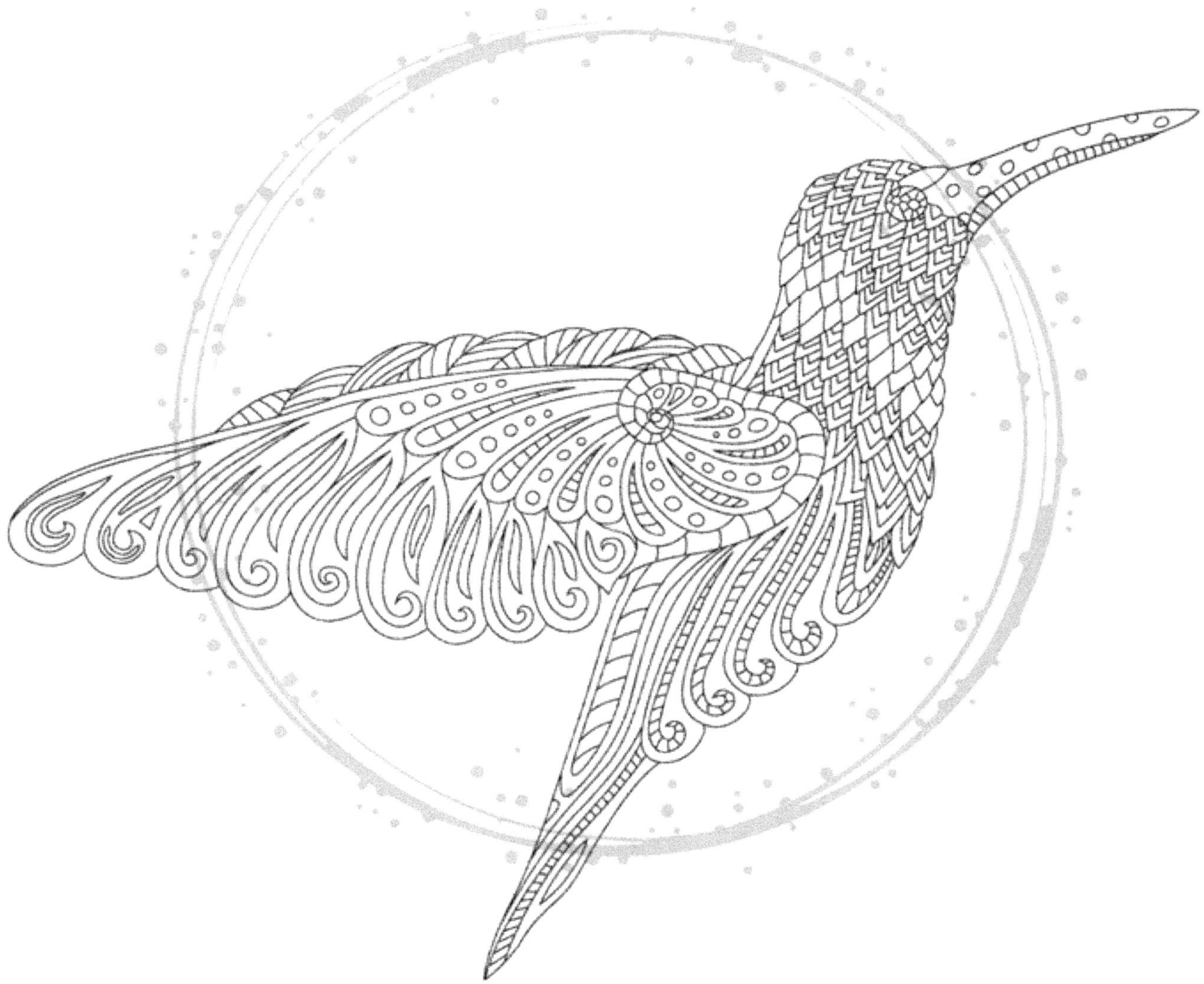

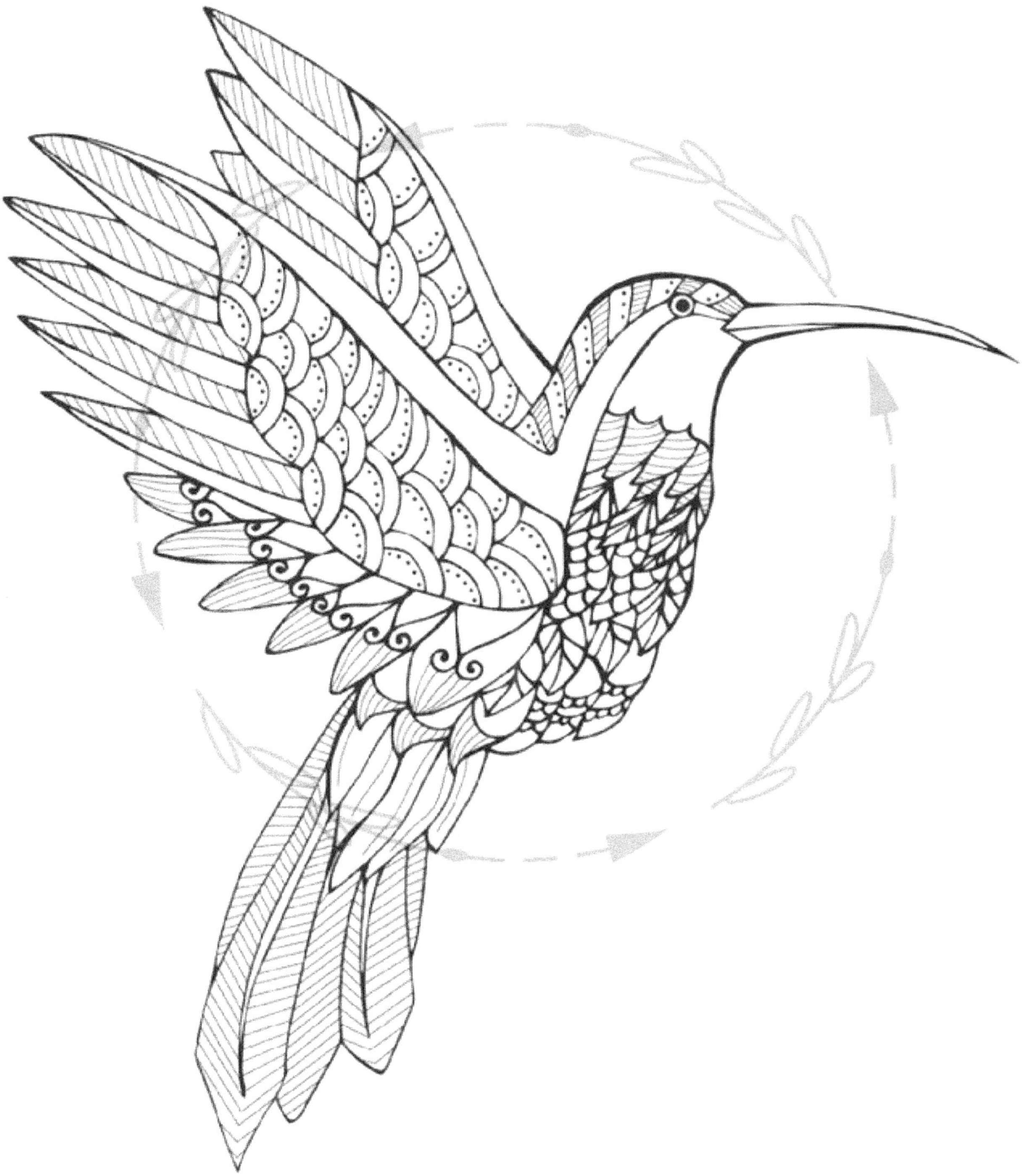

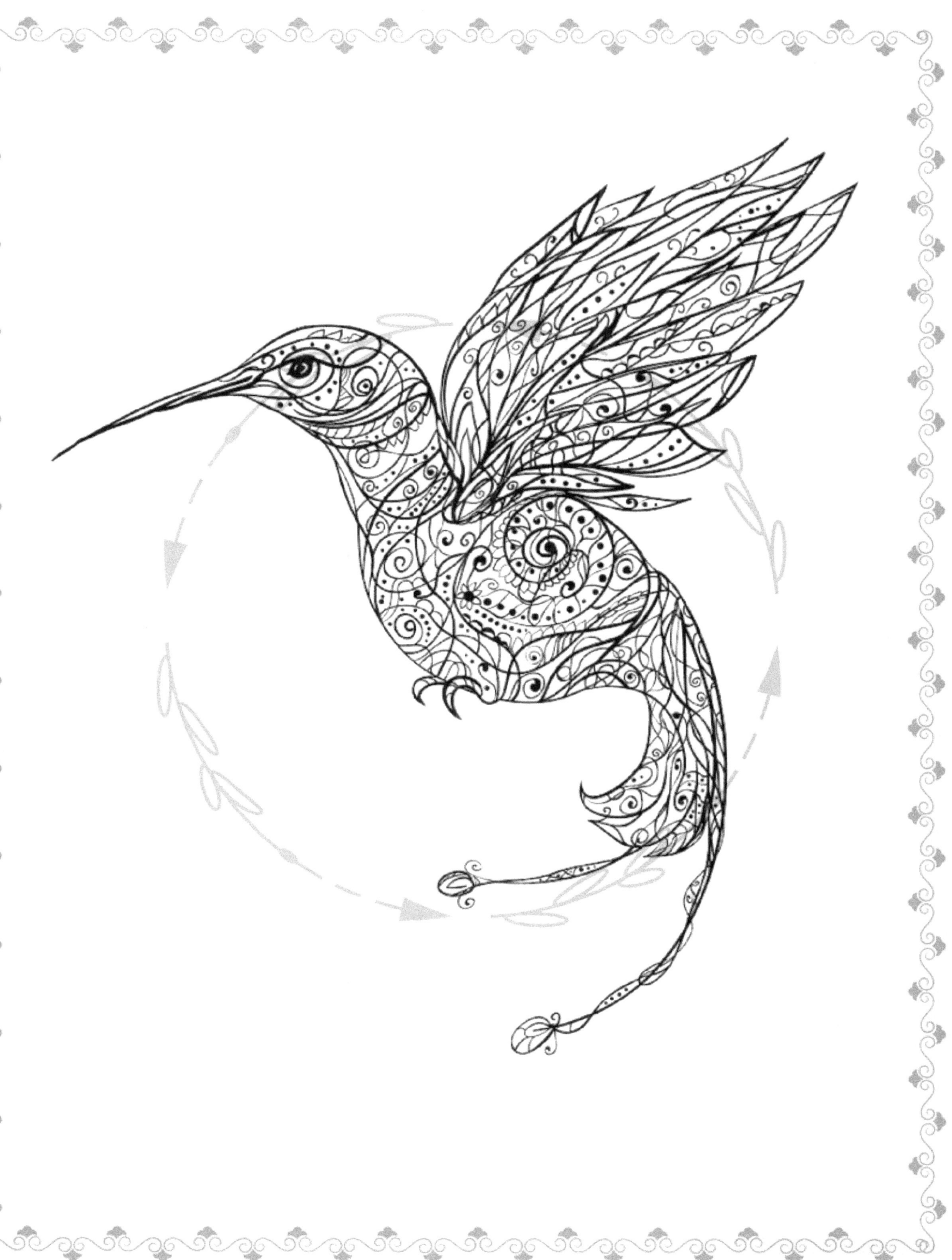

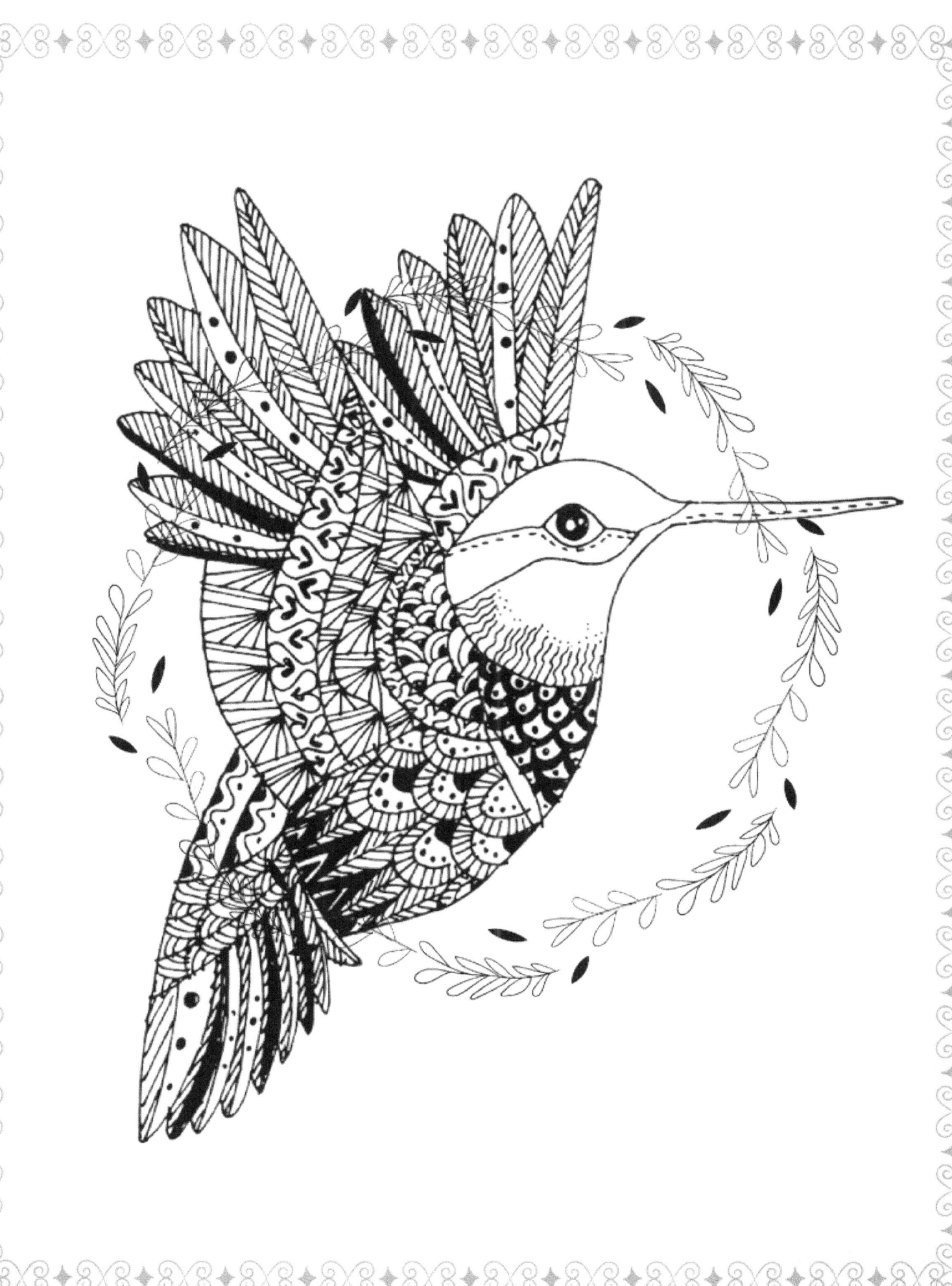

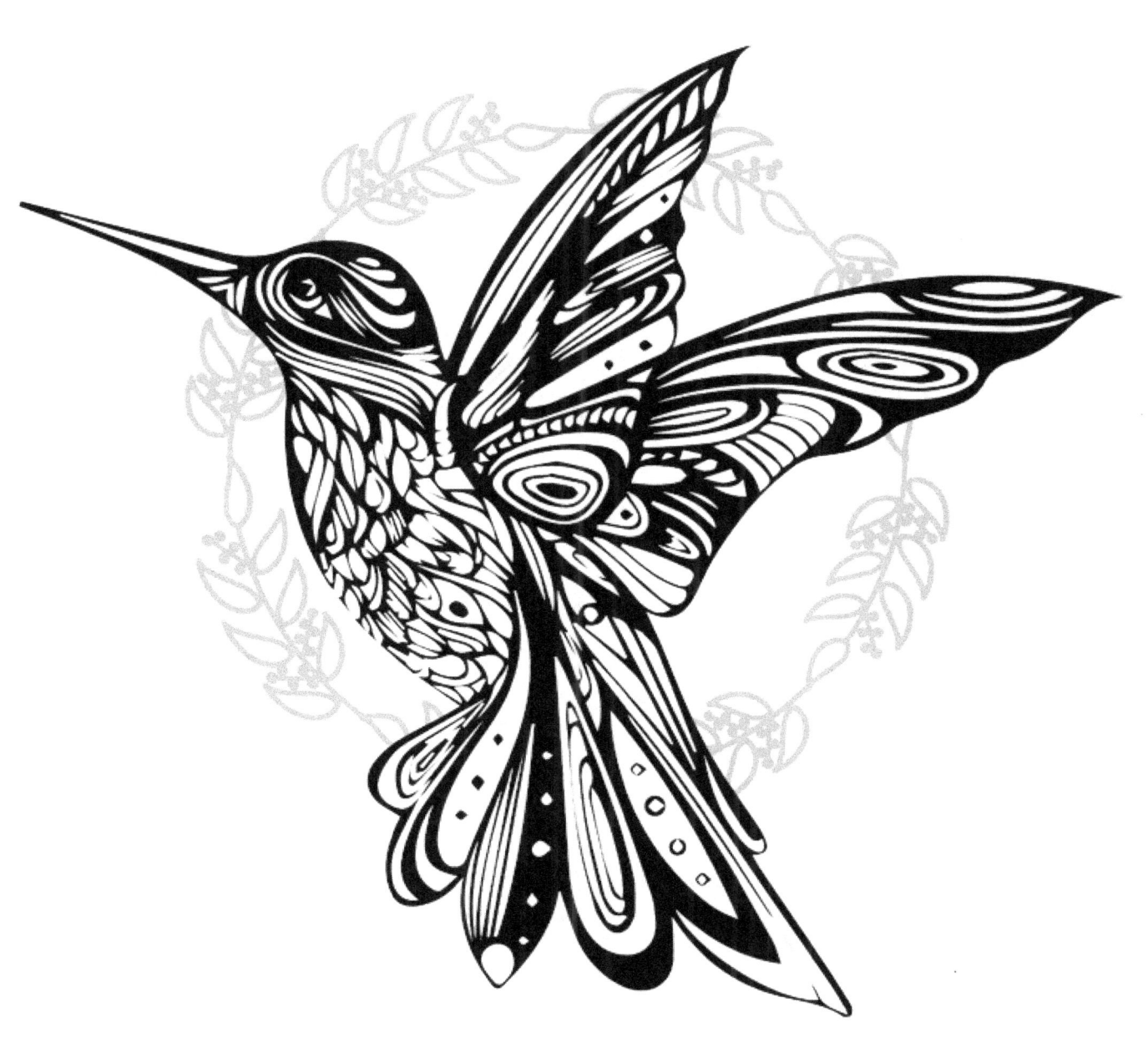

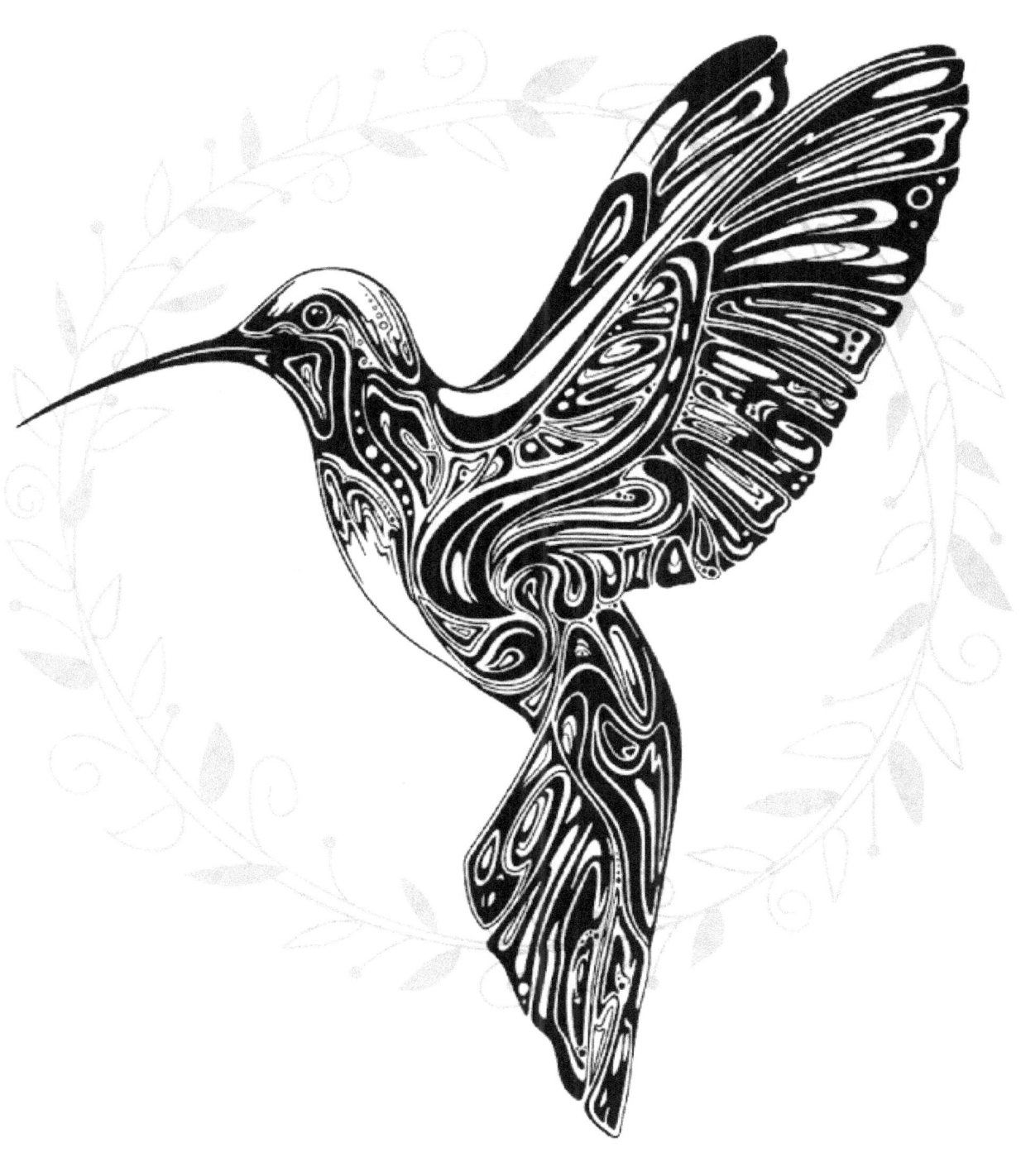

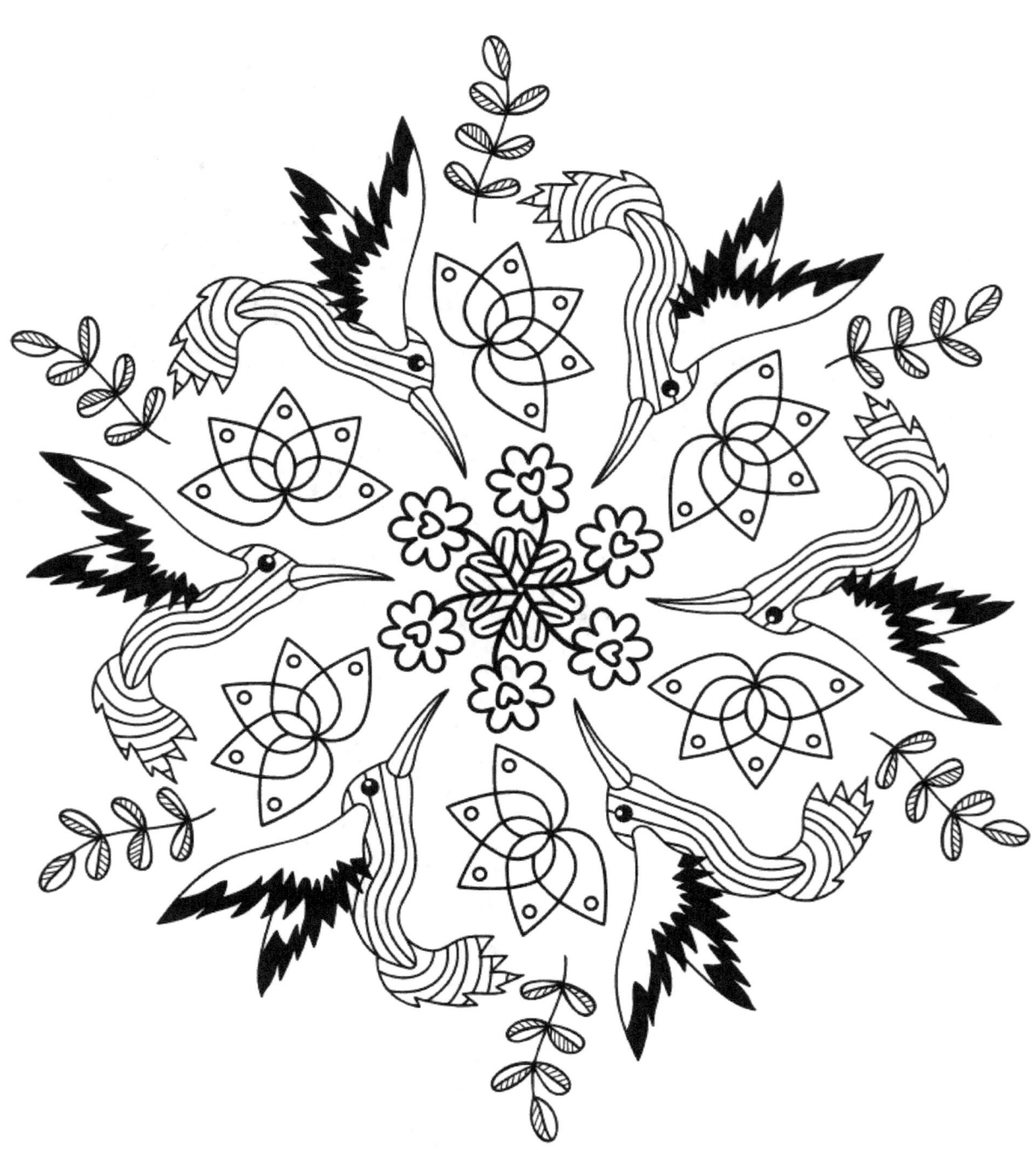

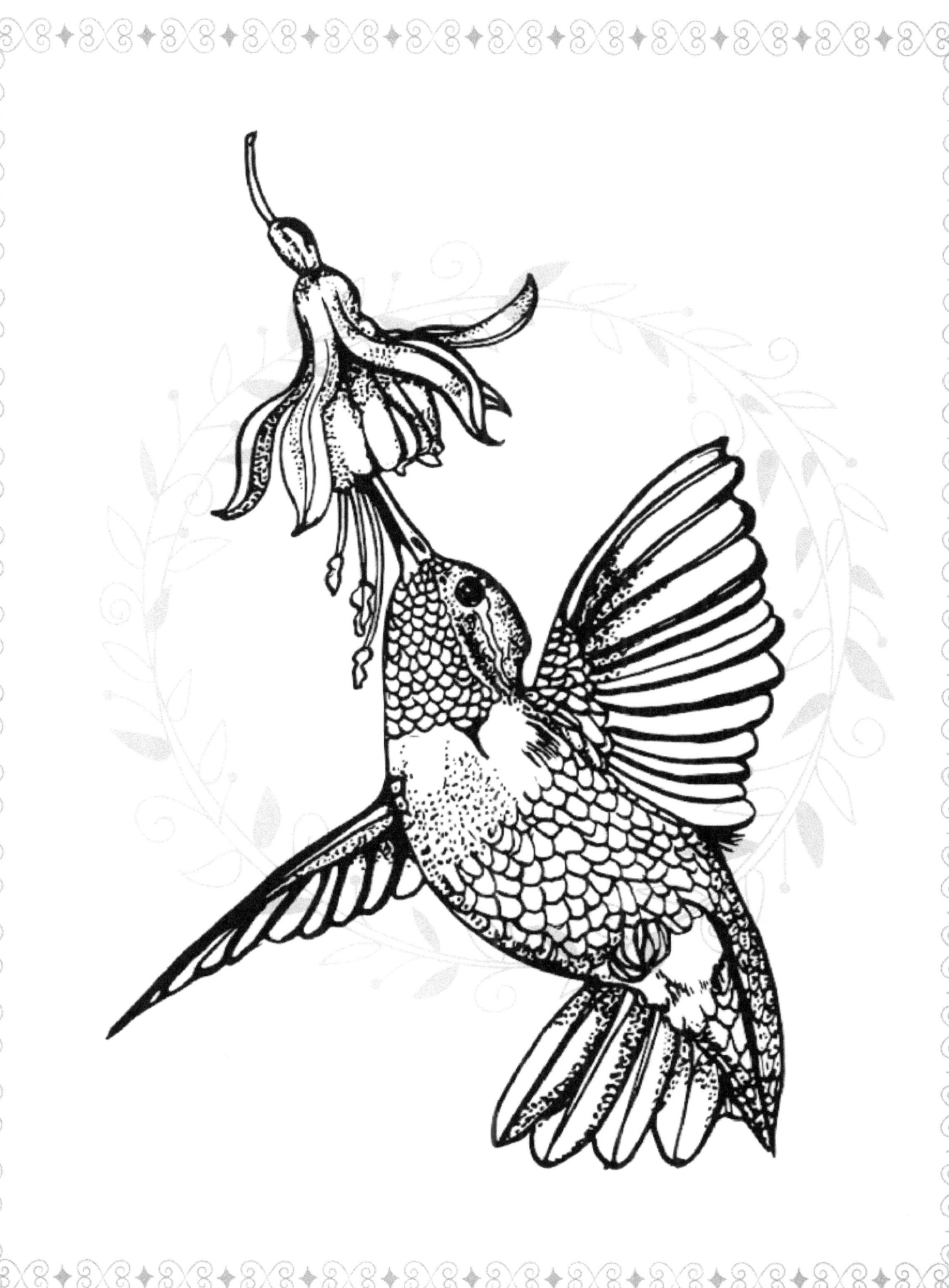

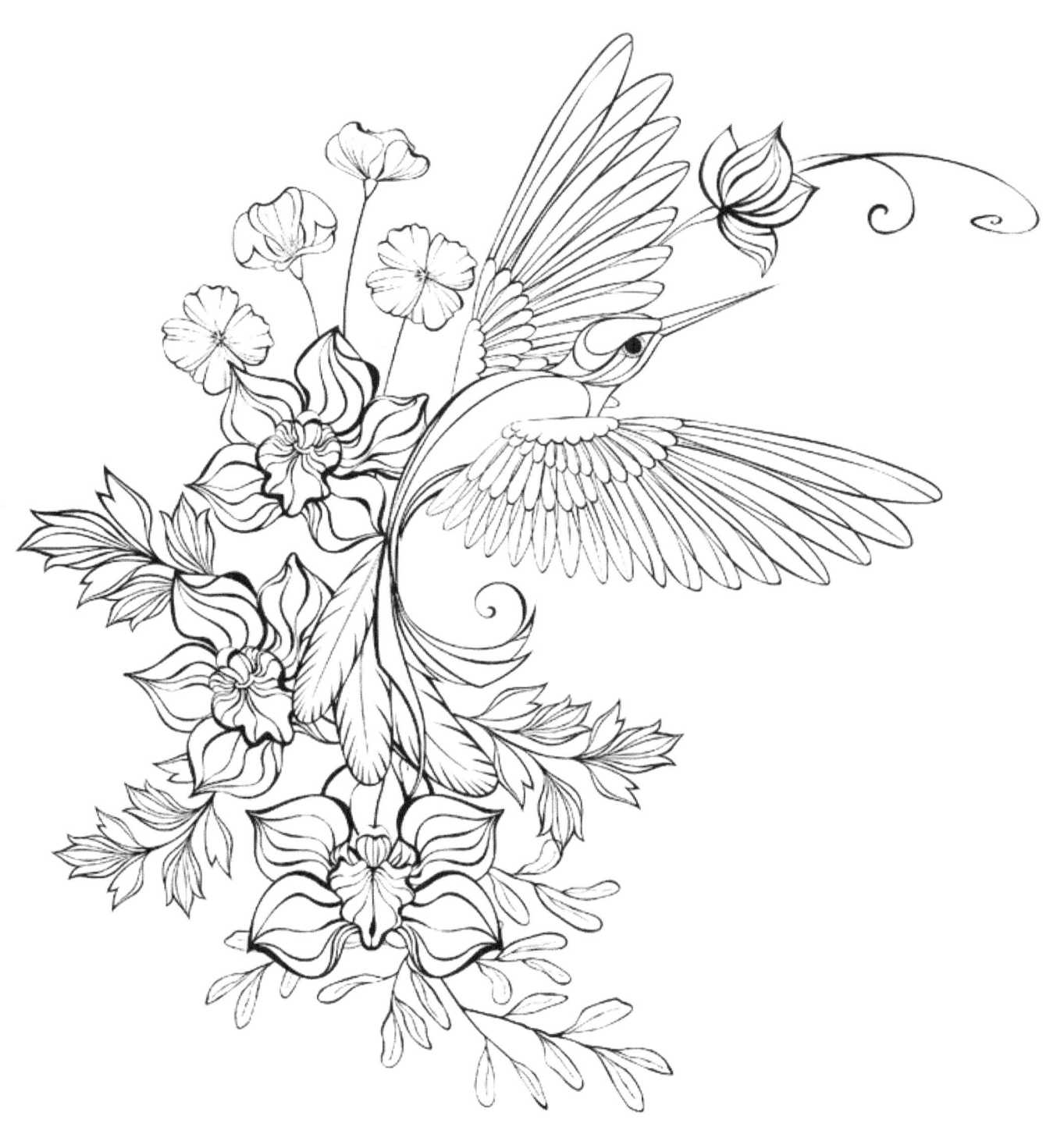

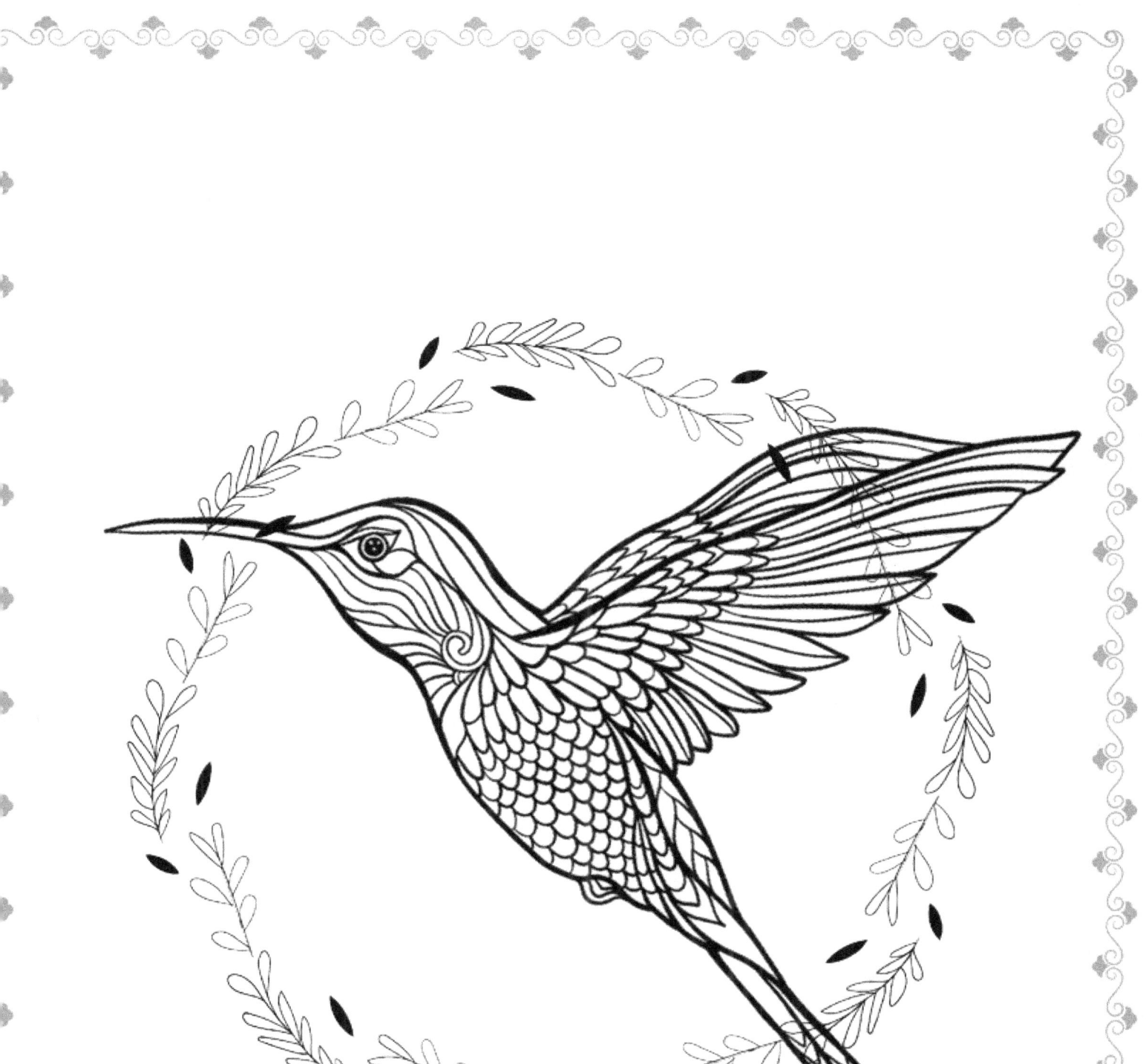

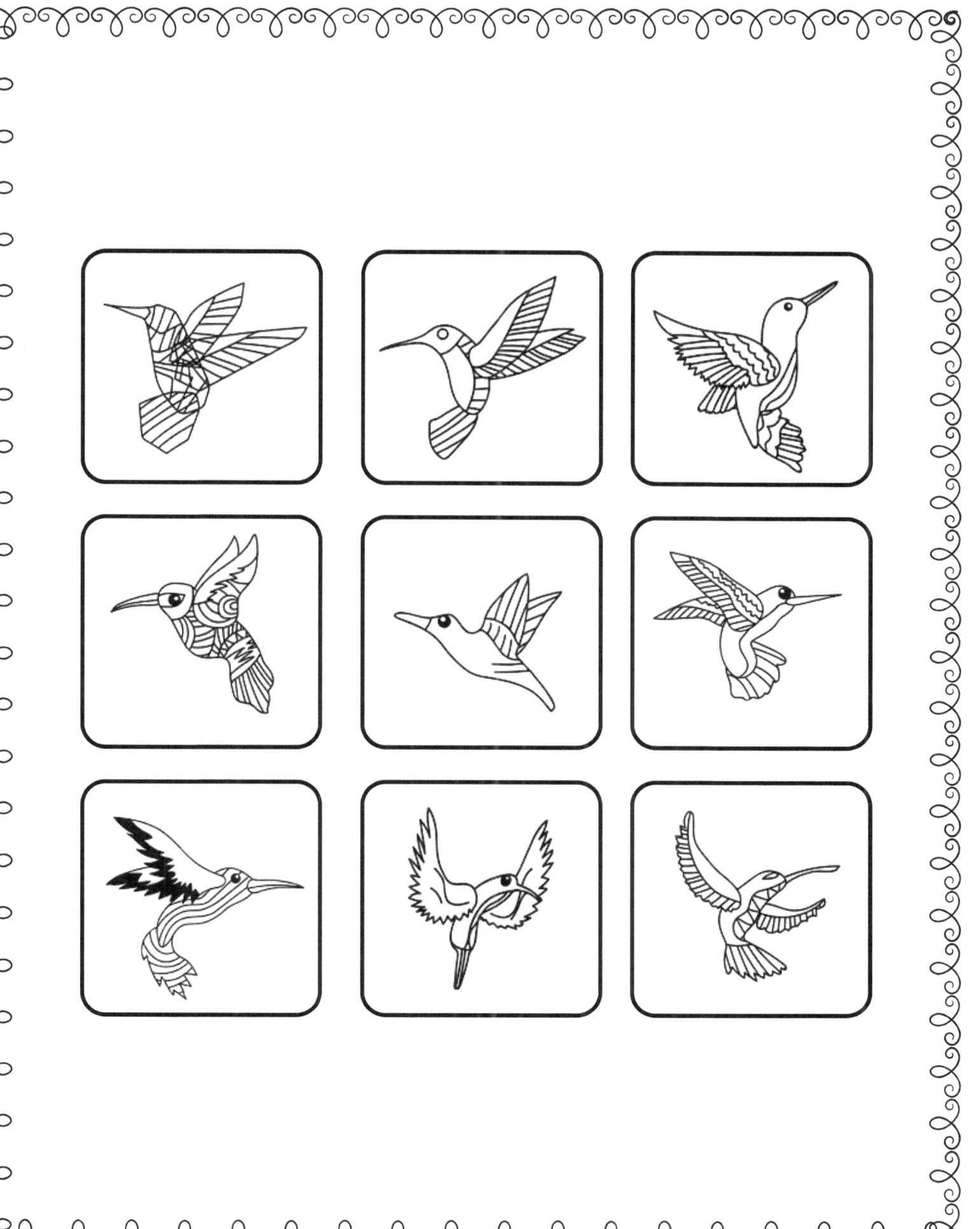

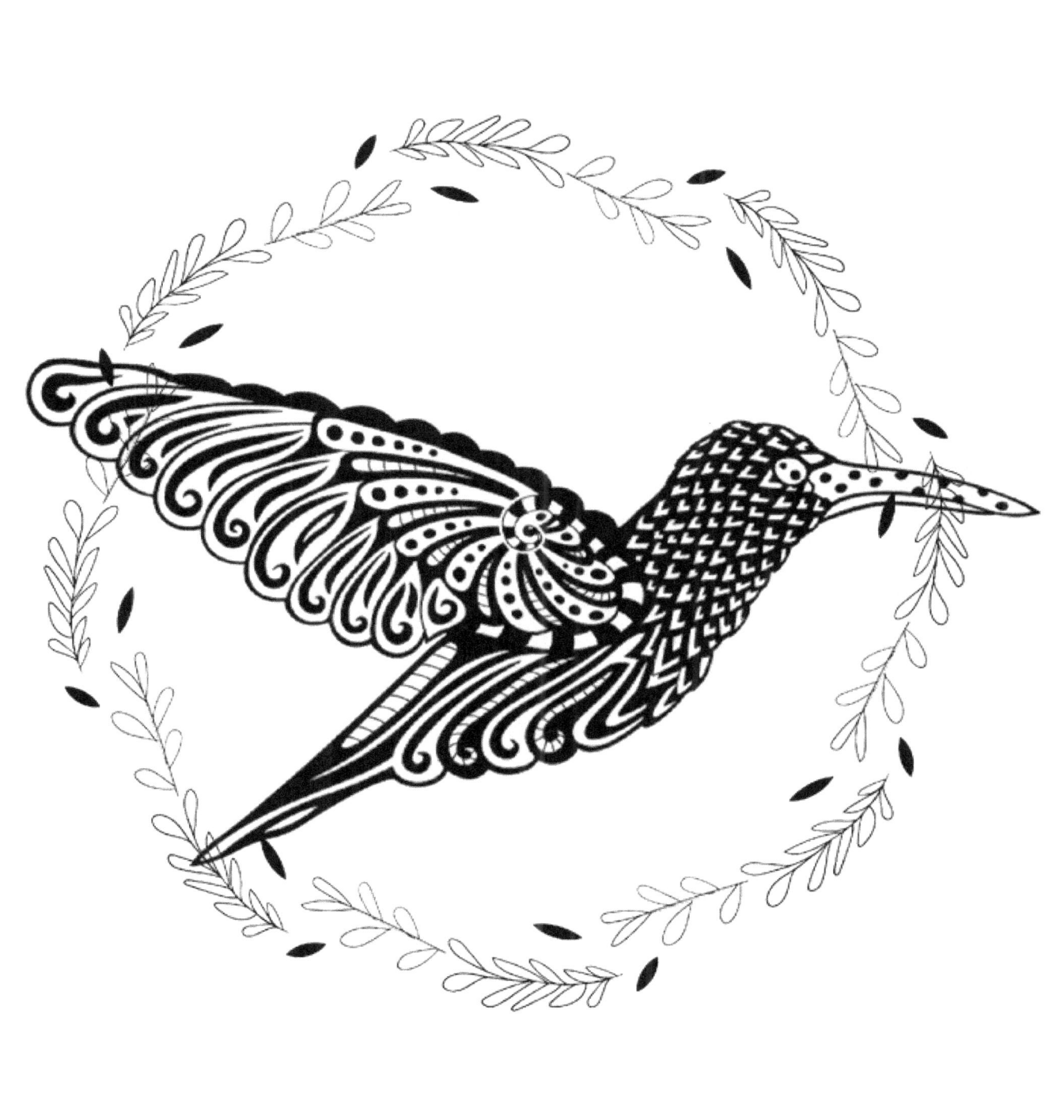

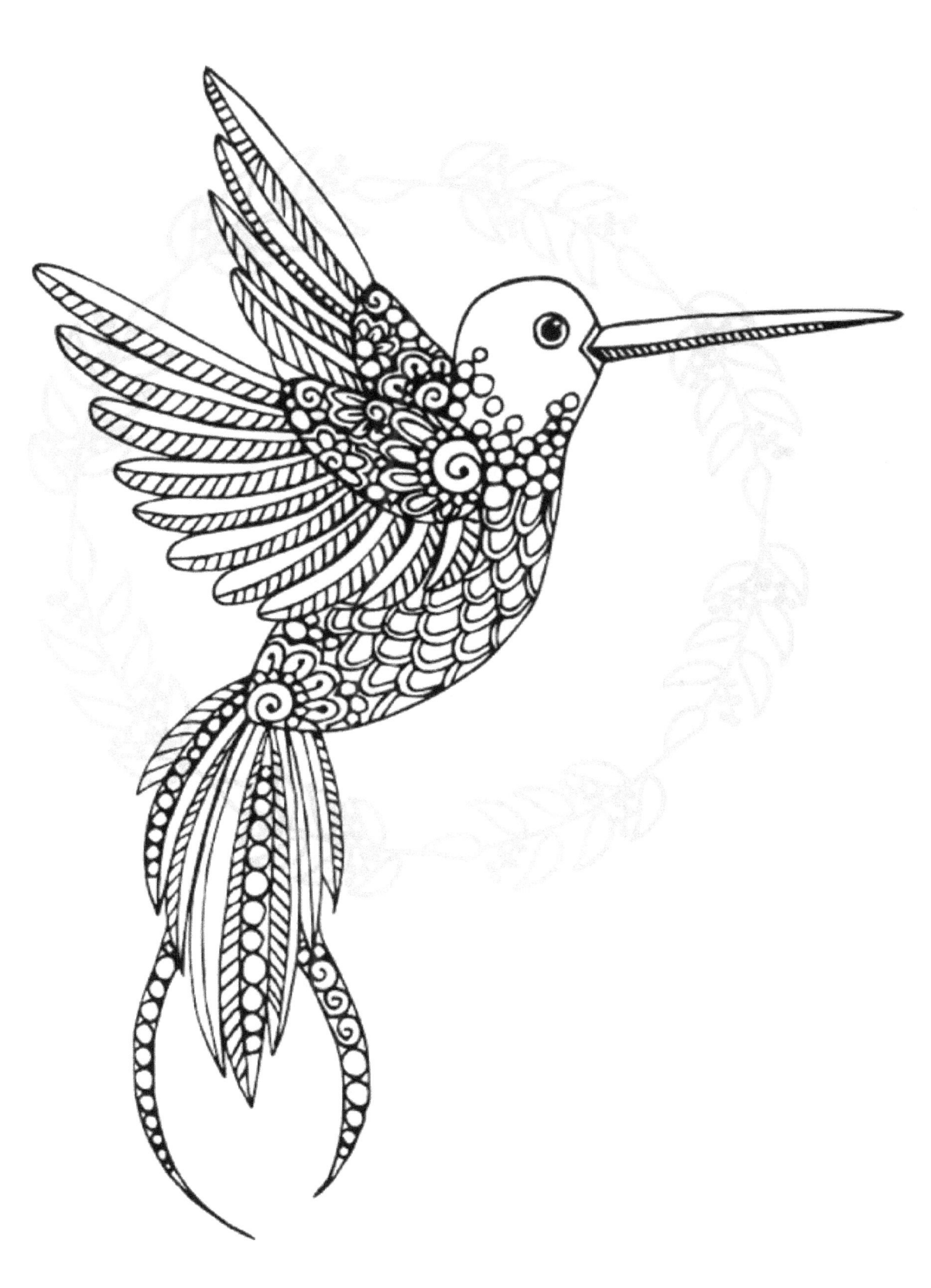

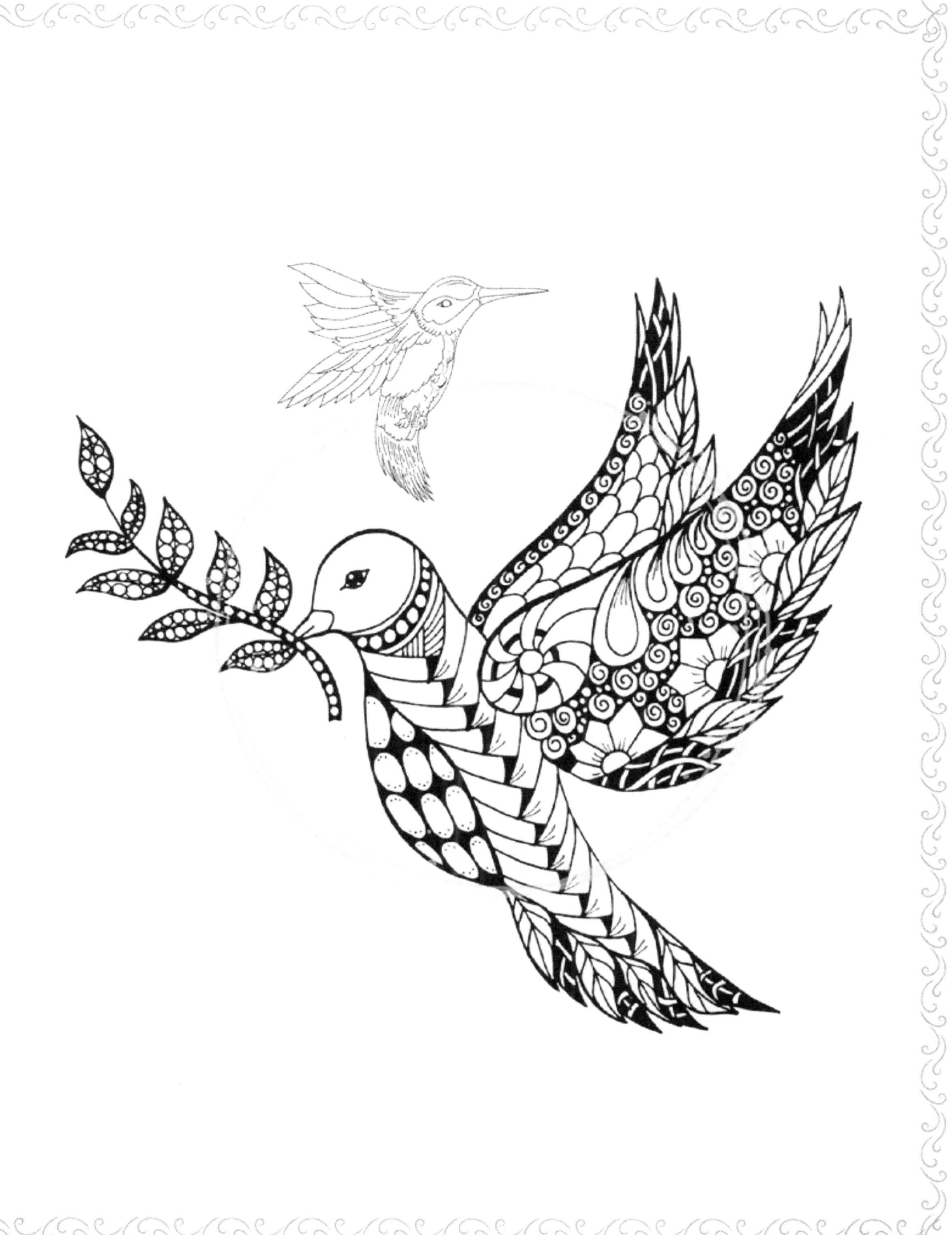

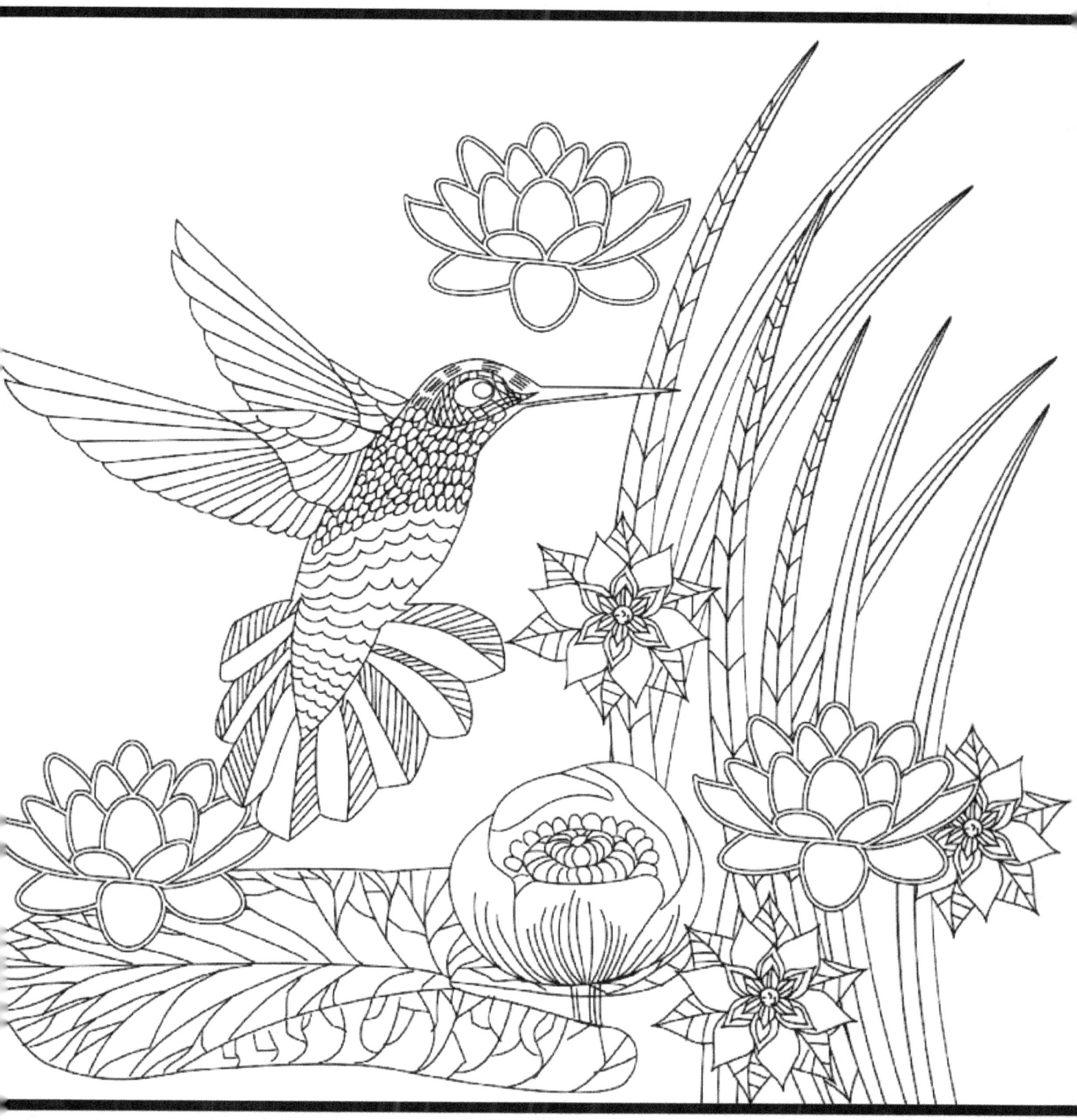

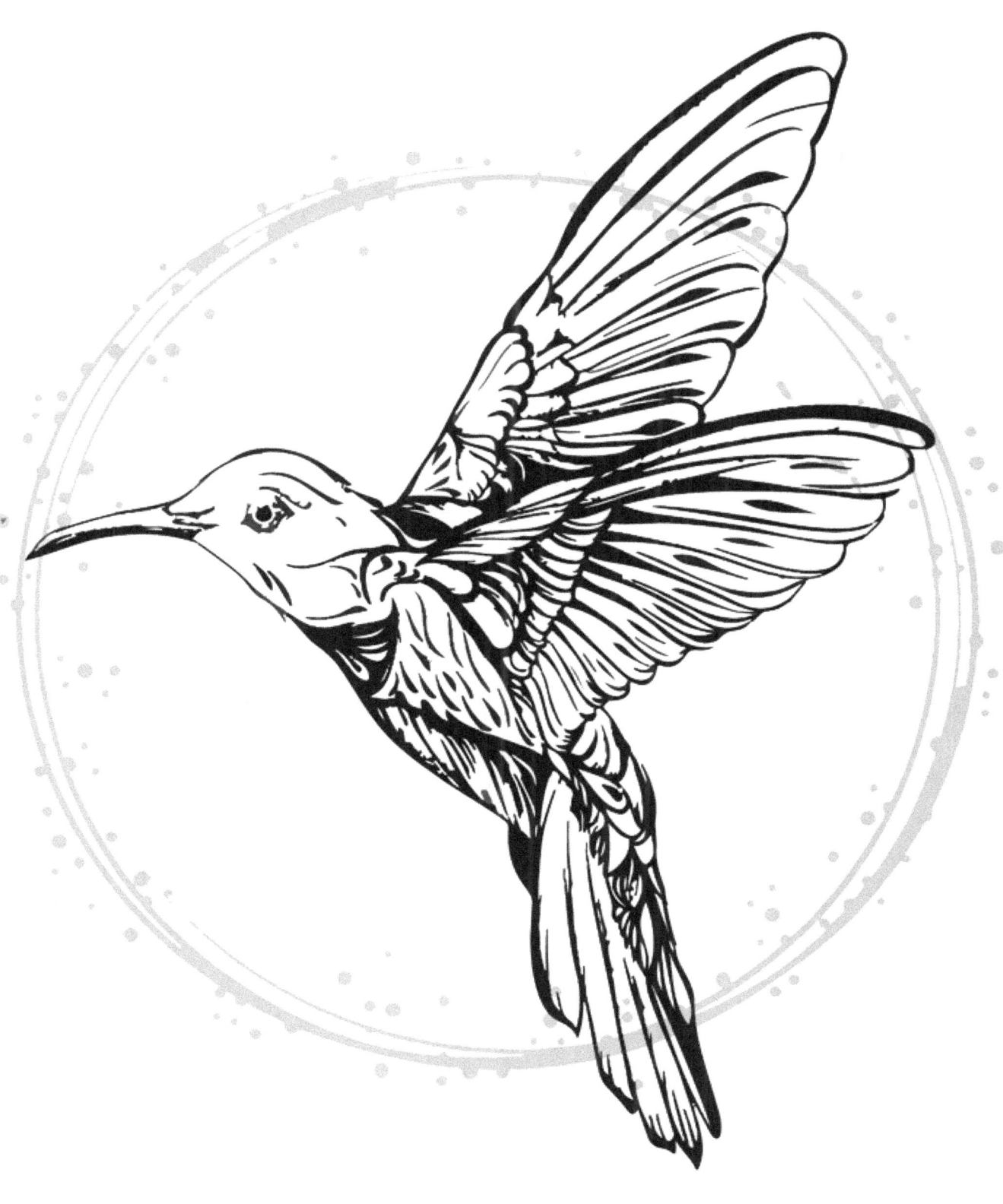

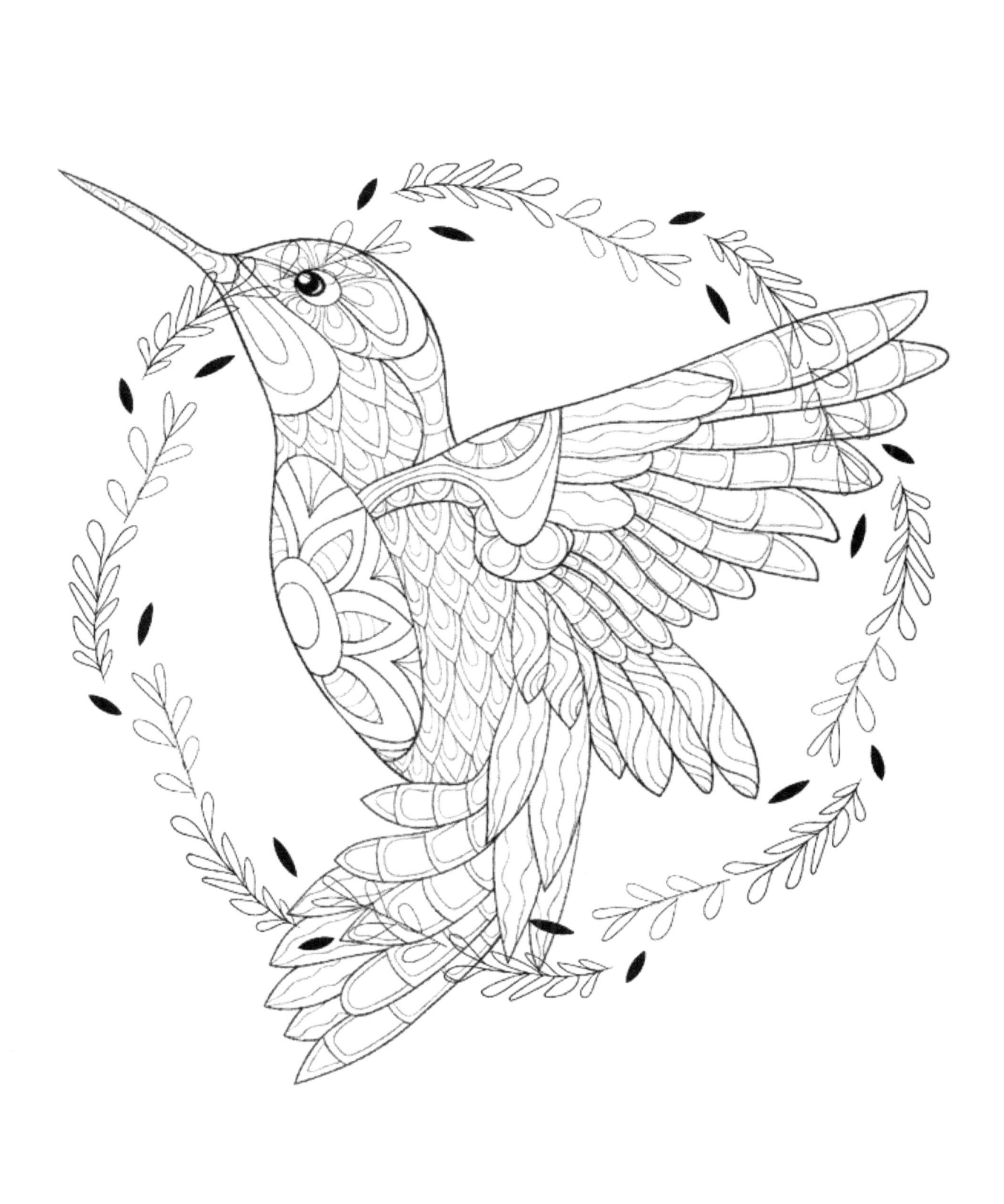

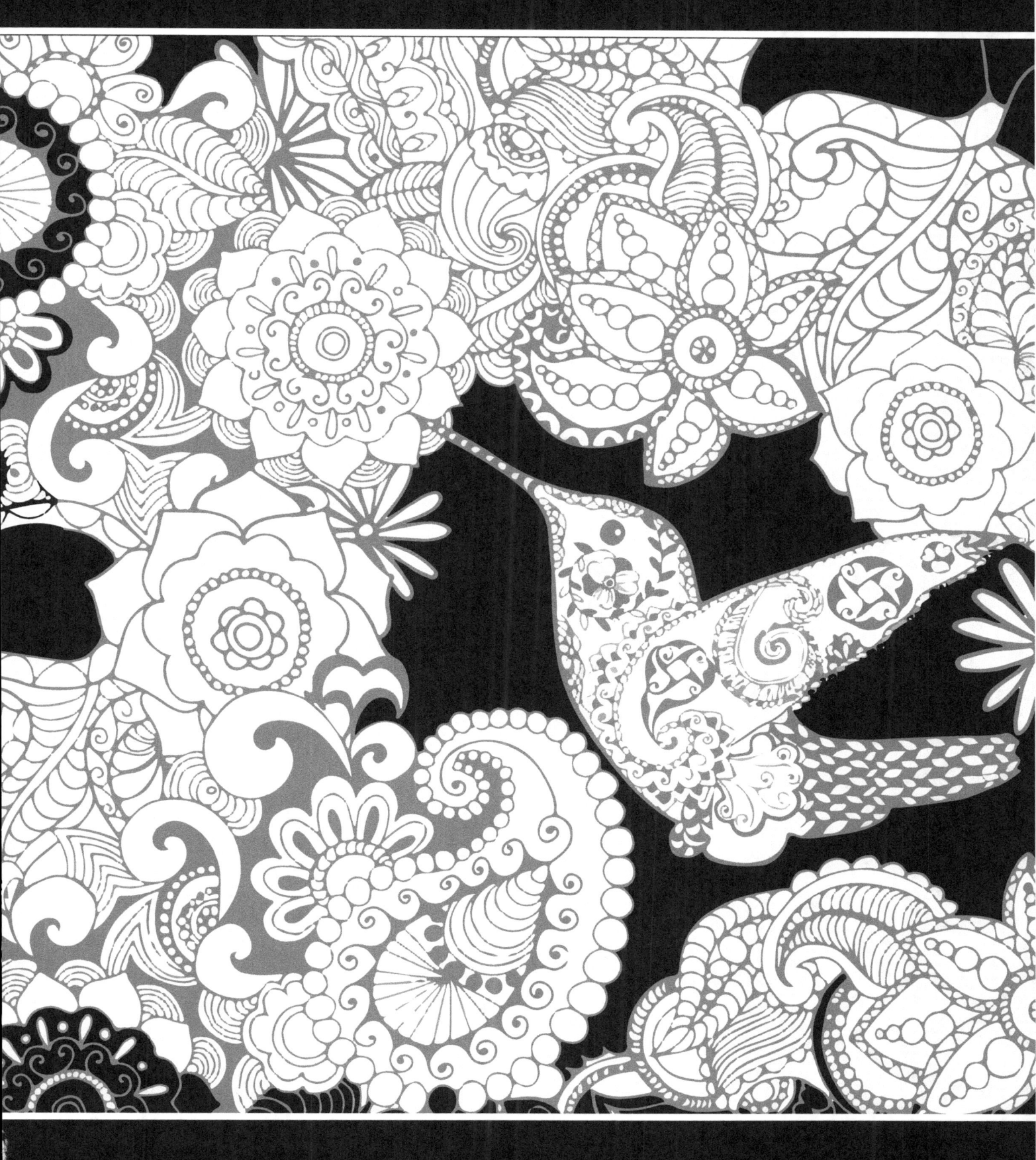

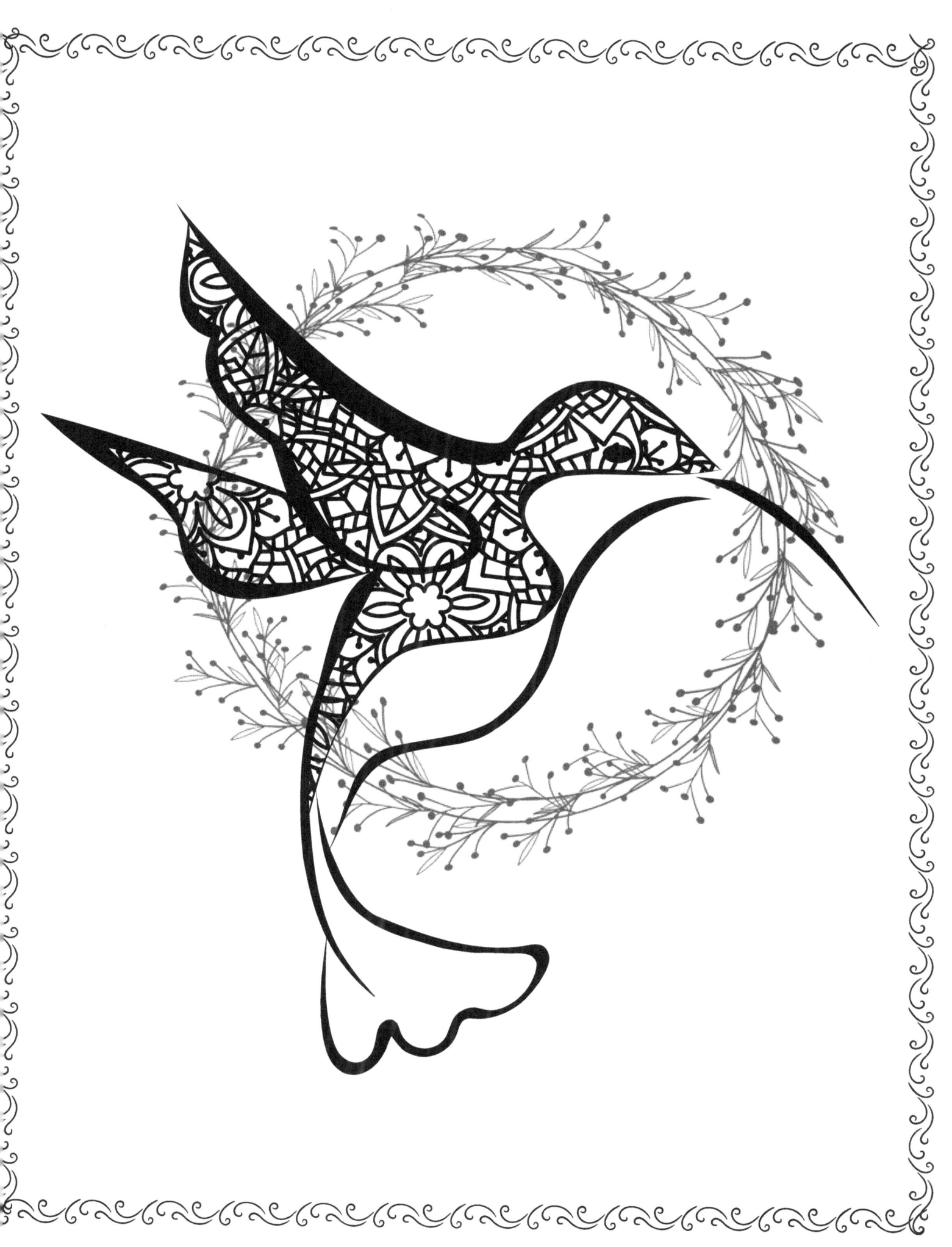

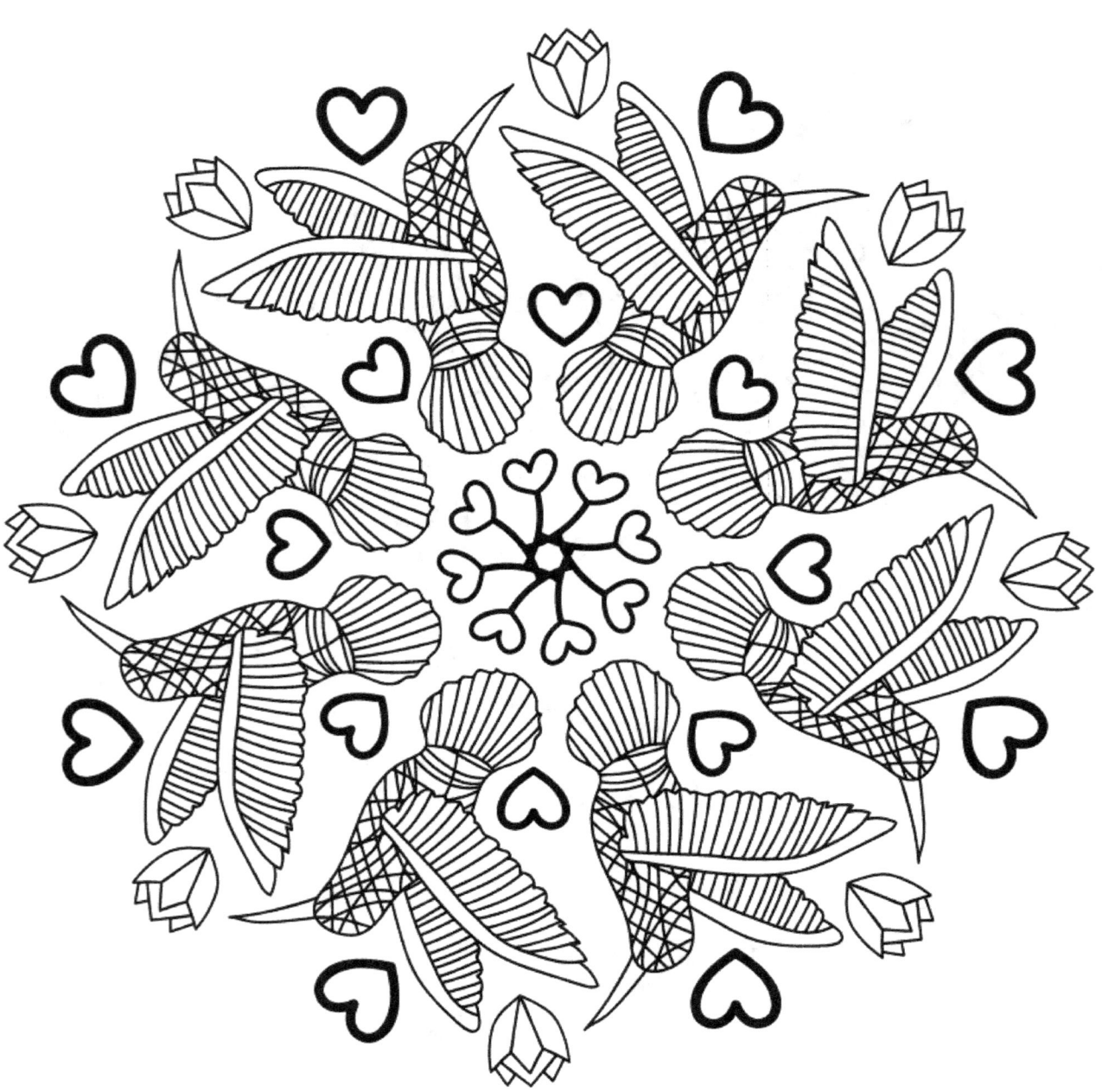

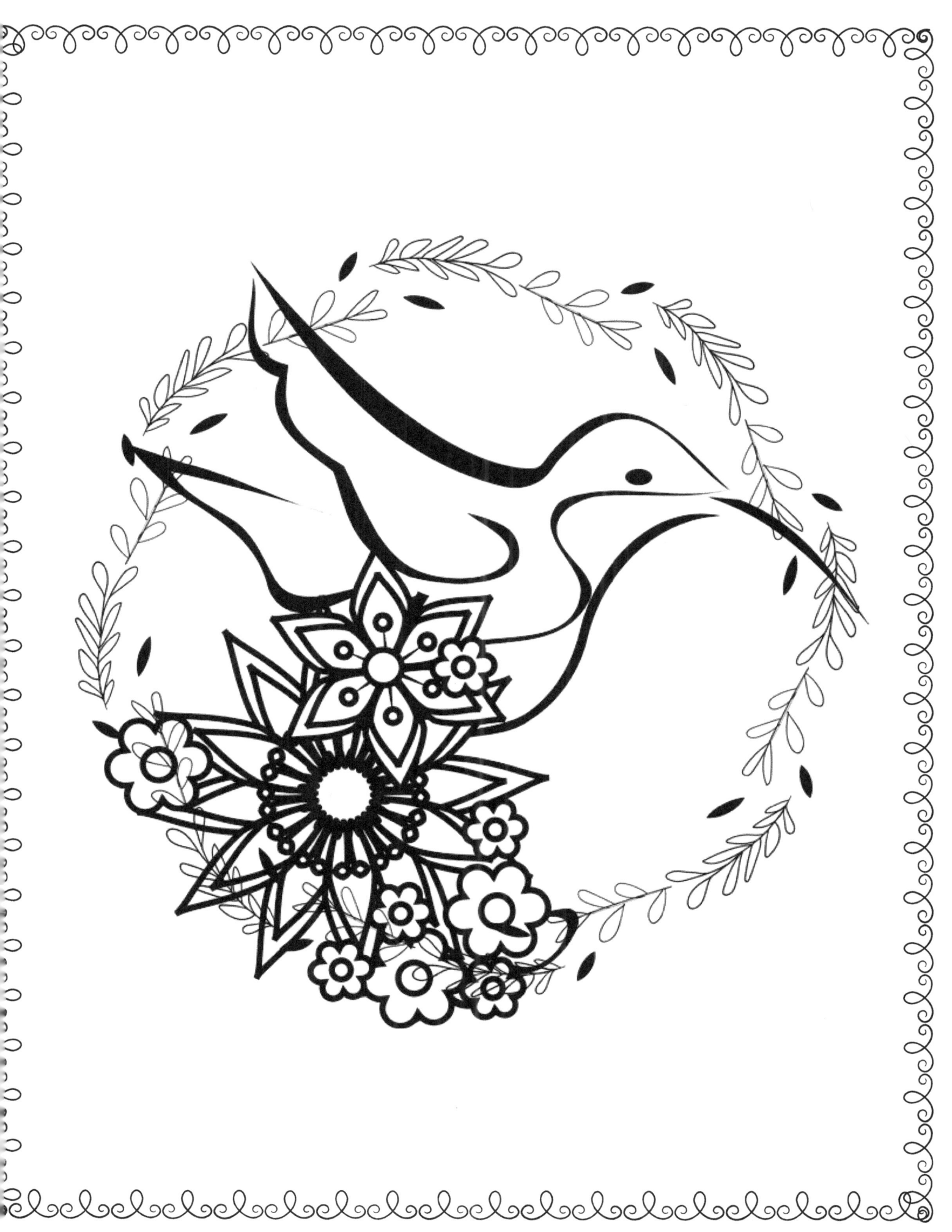

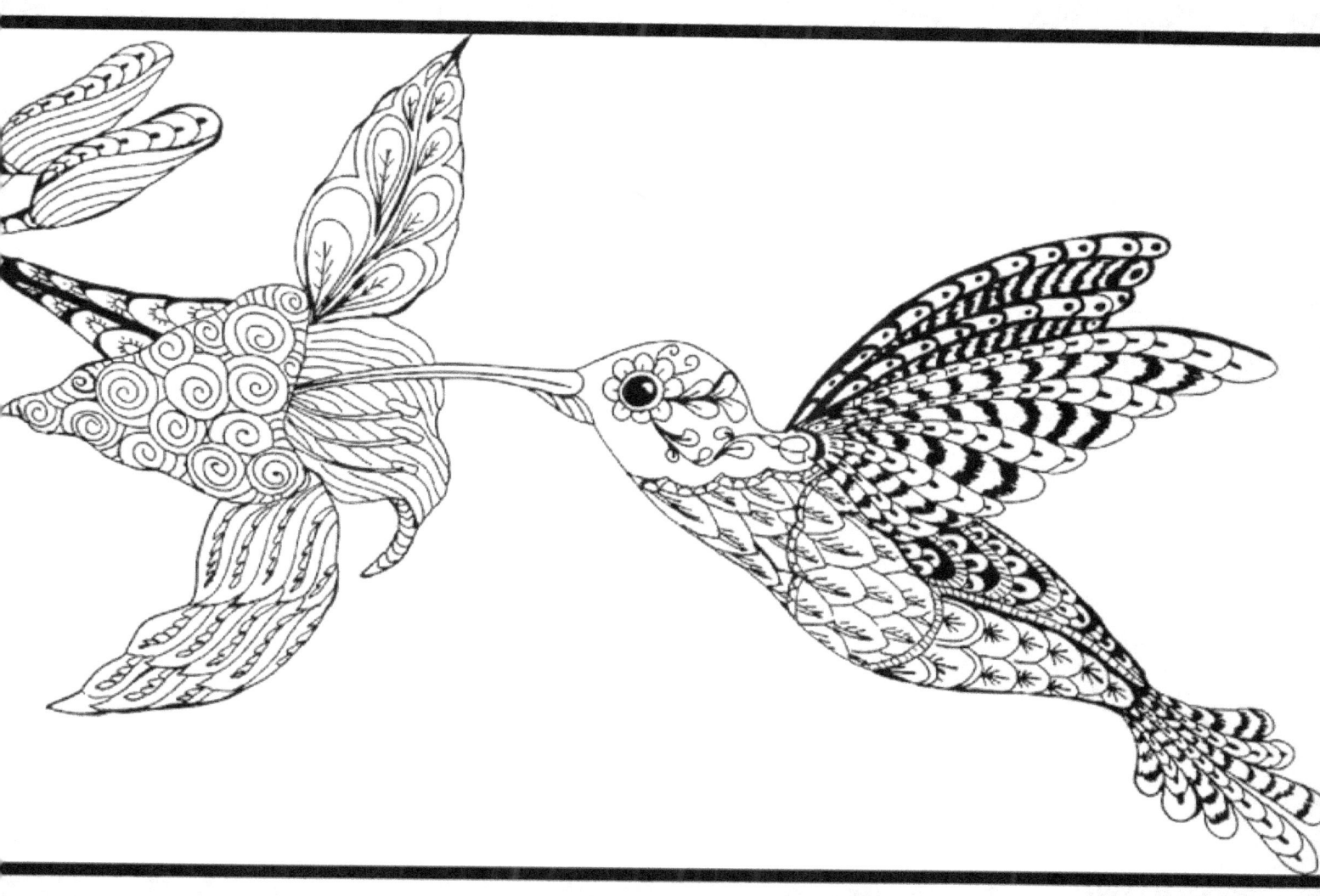

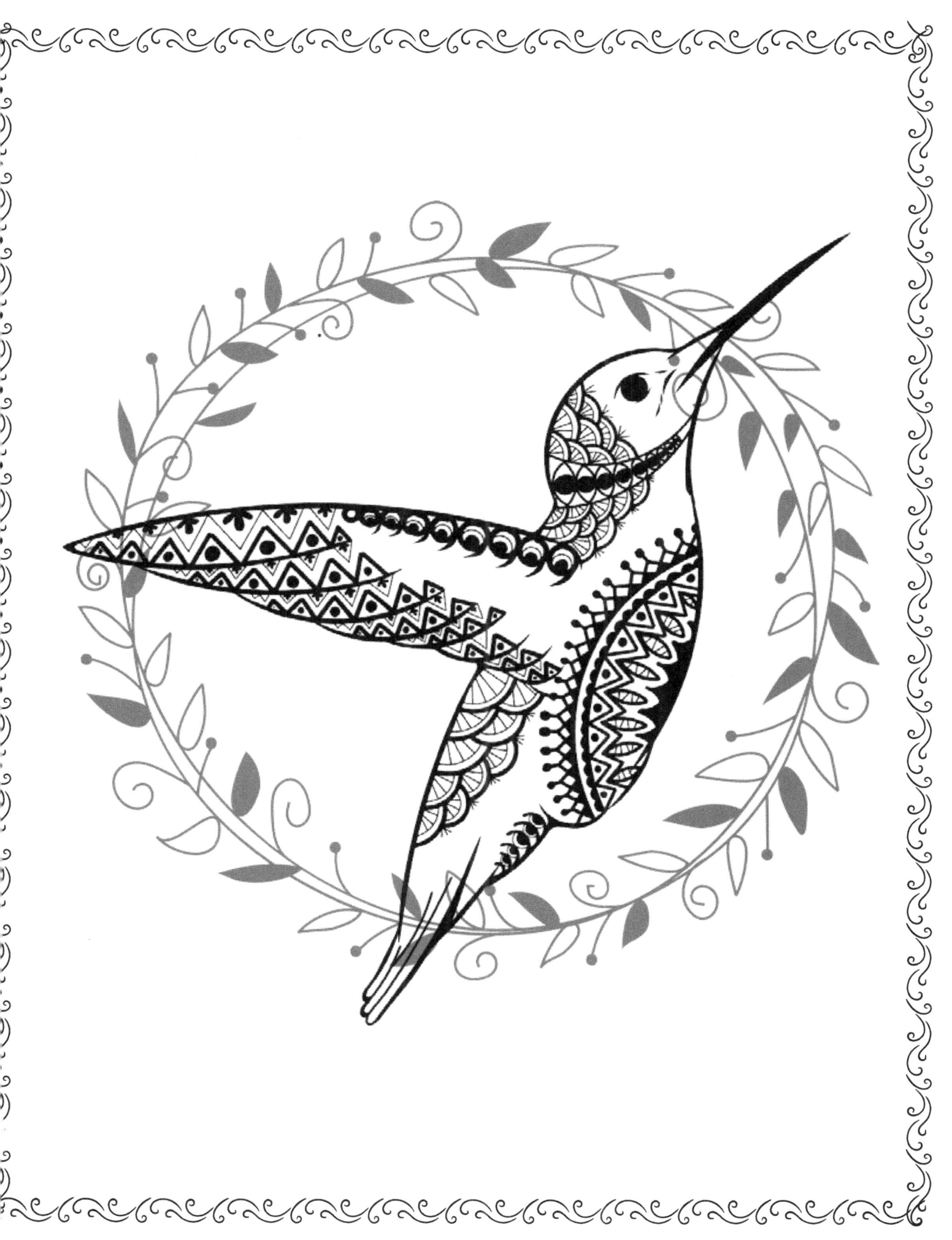

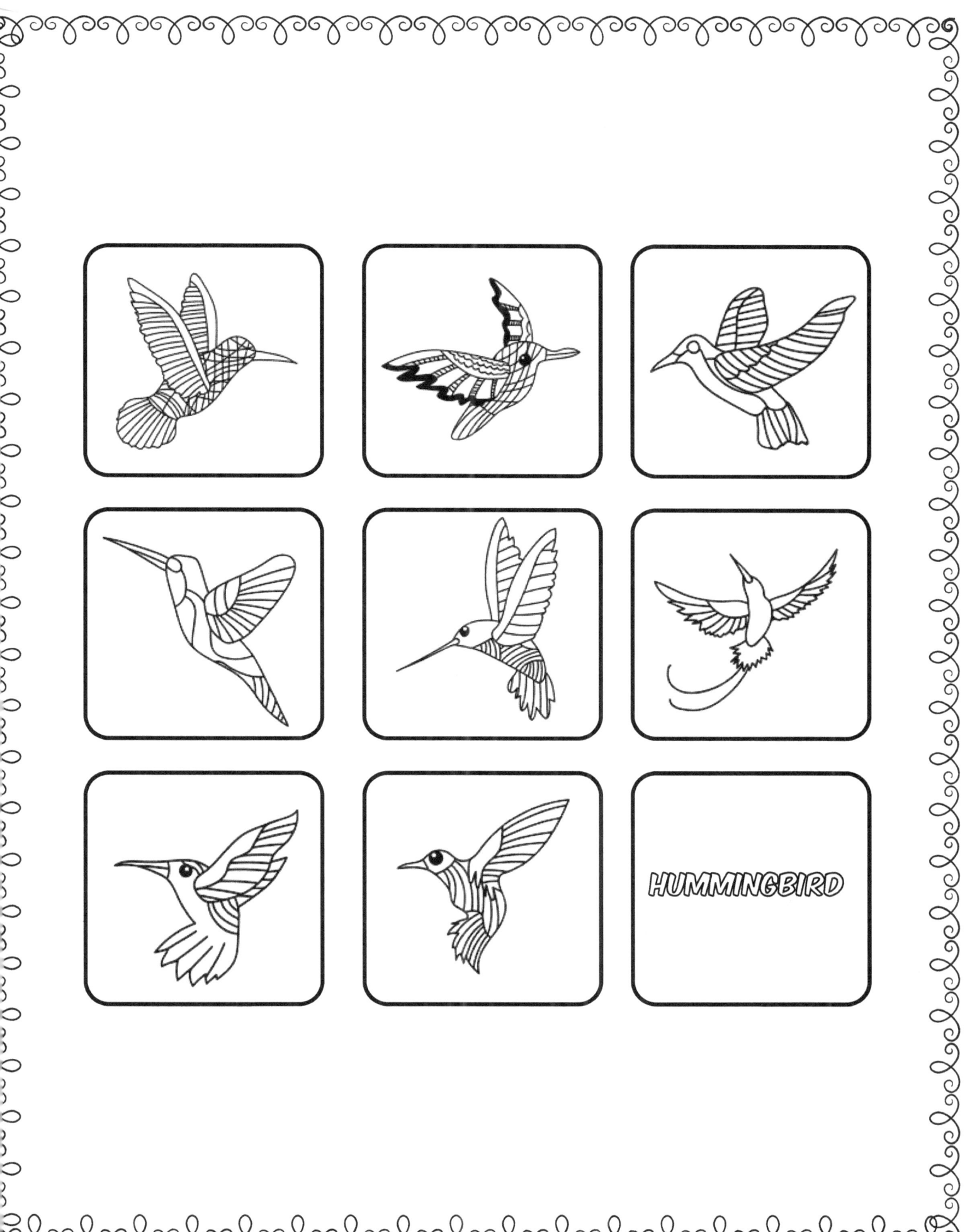
HUMMINGBIRD

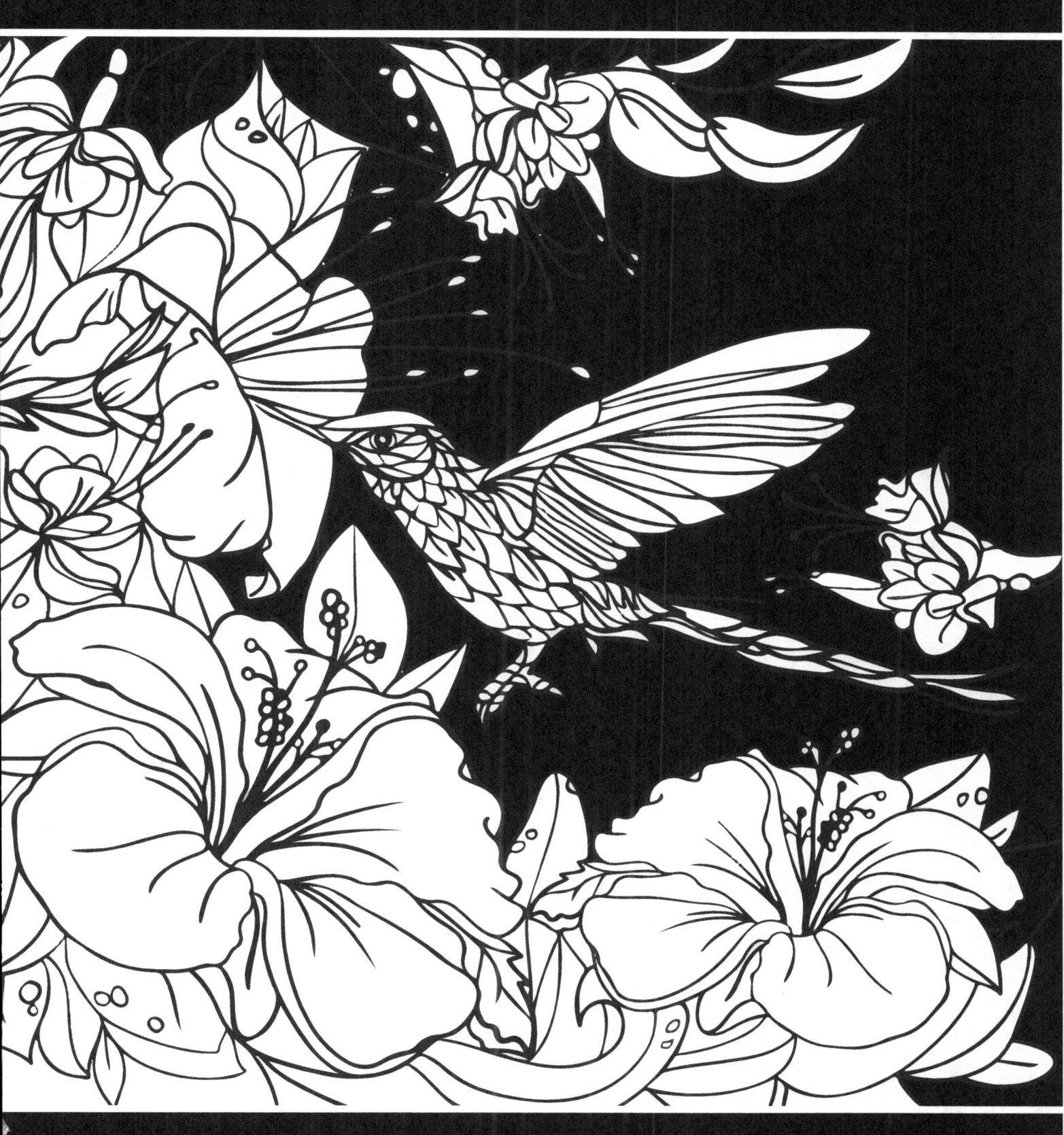

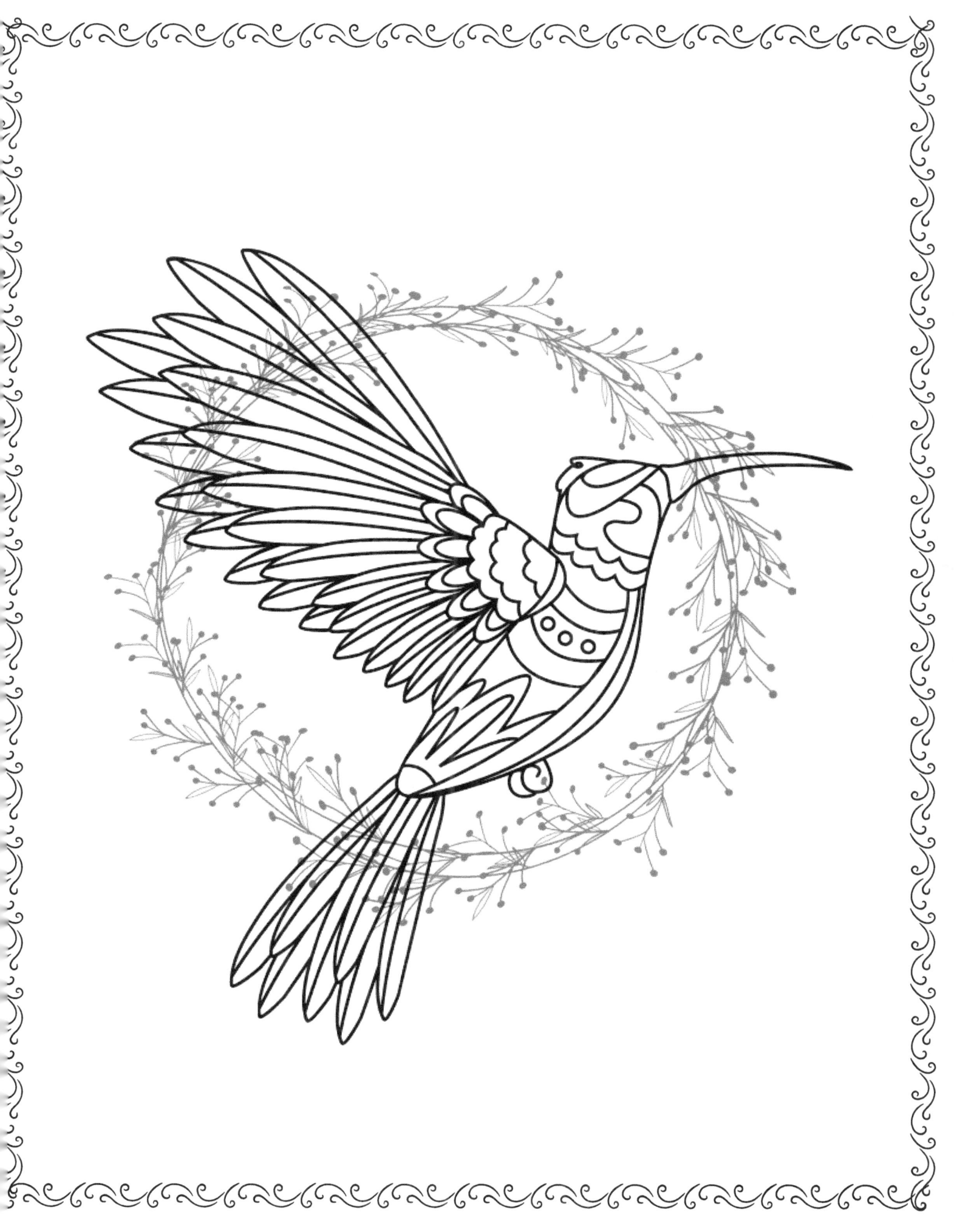

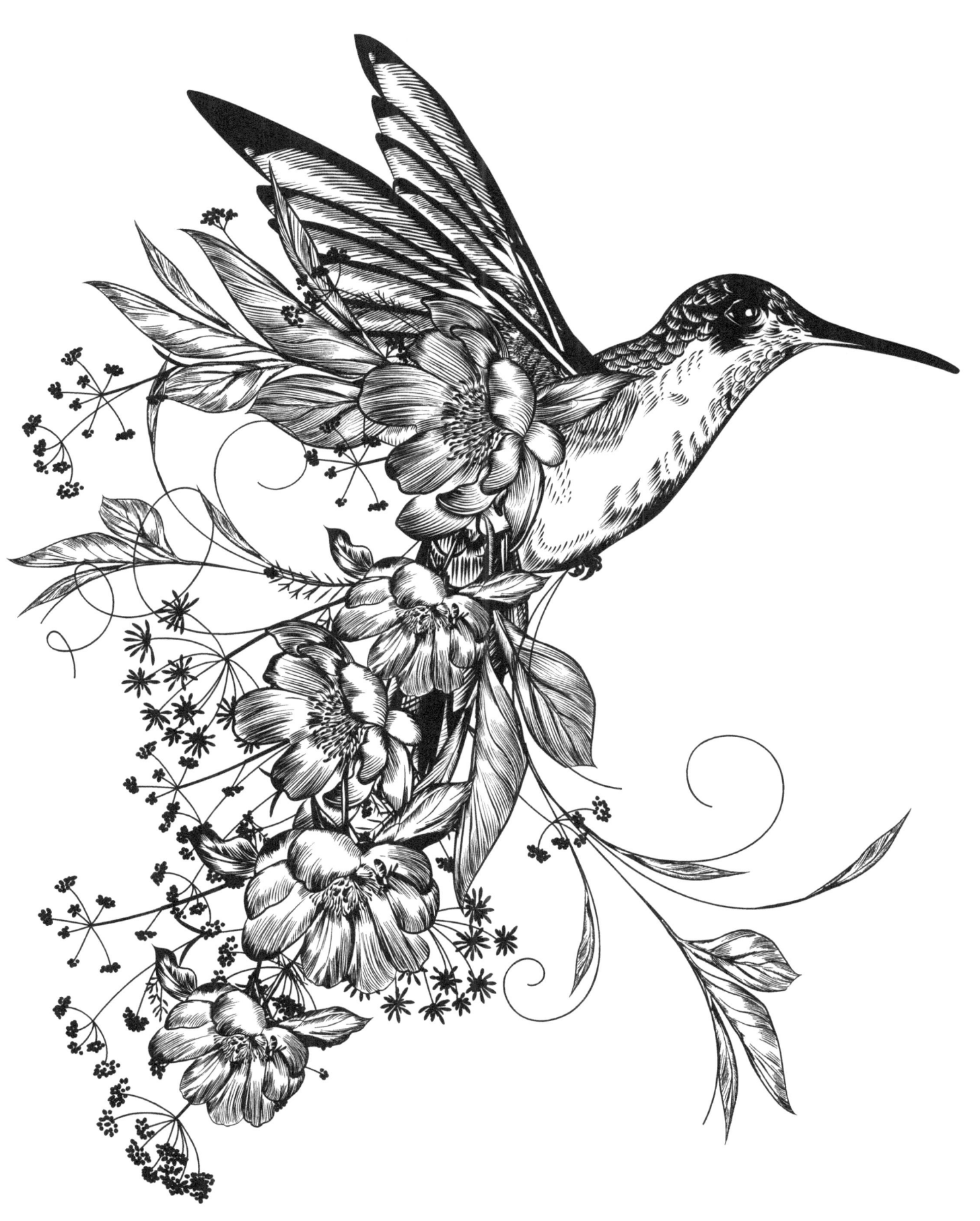

Thank you for supporting

TRODERO ART

I aim to make sure my customers have the most enjoyable and relaxing coloring experience possible, and I would love to hear your feedback! Please leave a review on Amazon, that means alot to me.